What about the Children?

What about the Children?

Five Values for Multiracial Families

NICOLE DOYLEY

WESTMINSTER JOHN KNOX PRESS
LOUISVILLE • KENTUCKY

© 2025 Nicole Doyley
Foreword © 2025 Westminster John Knox Press

First edition
Published by Westminster John Knox Press
Louisville, Kentucky

Published in association with the Books & Such Literary Agency, www.booksandsuch.com.

25 26 27 28 29 30 31 32 33 34—10 9 8 7 6 5 4 3 2 1

All rights reserved. No part of this book may be reproduced or transmitted in any form or by any means, electronic or mechanical, including photocopying, recording, or by any information storage or retrieval system, without permission in writing from the publisher. For information, address Westminster John Knox Press, 100 Witherspoon Street, Louisville, Kentucky 40202-1396. Or contact us online at www.wjkbooks.com.

Unless otherwise indicated, Scripture quotations are from the New King James Version®. Copyright © 1982 by Thomas Nelson. Used by permission. All rights reserved. Scripture quotations marked NIV are from the Holy Bible, New International Version. Copyright © 1973, 1978, 1984, 2011 by Biblica, Inc.® Used by permission of Zondervan. All rights reserved worldwide. Scripture quotations marked NASB are taken from the New American Standard Bible, copyright © 1960, 1971, 1977, 1995, 2020 by The Lockman Foundation. All rights reserved. Scripture quotations marked NLT are taken from the *Holy Bible,* New Living Translation, copyright © 1996, 2004, 2015 by Tyndale House Foundation. Used by permission of Tyndale House Publishers, Inc., Carol Stream, Illinois 60188. All rights reserved. Scripture quotations marked MSG are taken from *The Message,* copyright © 1993, 2002, 2018 by Eugene H. Peterson. Used by permission of NavPress. All rights reserved. Represented by Tyndale House Publishers, Inc.

Book design by Drew Stevens
Cover design by Kevin van der Leek

Library of Congress Cataloging-in-Publication Data

Names: Doyley, Nicole, author.
Title: What about the children? : five values for multiracial families /
  Nicole Doyley.
Description: First edition. | Louisville, Kentucky : Westminster John Knox
  Press, [2025] | Summary: "Provides insight and guidance for parents of
  multiracial children (or children whose race does not match their
  parents', in the case of transracial adoption) to help their children
  grow up with a strong sense of identity and comfort in navigating the
  different cultures that are part of their identity"-- Provided by
  publisher.
Identifiers: LCCN 2024054571 (print) | LCCN 2024054572 (ebook) | ISBN
  9780664268992 (paperback) | ISBN 9781646984183 (ebook)
Subjects: LCSH: Multiracial children--Ethnic identity. | Multiracial
  children--Attitudes. | Race awareness in children. | Child
  rearing--Religious aspects--Christianity.
Classification: LCC HQ777.9 .D69 2025 (print) | LCC HQ777.9 (ebook) | DDC
  649/.157--dc23/eng/20241226
LC record available at https://lccn.loc.gov/2024054571
LC ebook record available at https://lccn.loc.gov/2024054572

Most Westminster John Knox Press books are available at special quantity discounts when purchased in bulk by corporations, organizations, and special-interest groups. For more information, please e-mail SpecialSales@wjkbooks.com.

*To Marvin, Isaac, and Ben
and to my parents, Austin and Jane Leonard*

Contents

Foreword by Tasha Jun	ix
Introduction	1
1. What about the Children?	5
2. Color Matters	11

Value I–Awareness

3. Race, the One-Drop Rule, and Cultural Racism	19
4. Colorism	35

Value II–Humility

5. Cultural Shibboleths Matter	51
6. You Can't Do It Alone!	67

Value III–Diversity

7. The Problem with Homogeneity	83
8. The Beauty of Diversity	97

Value IV–Honesty

9. Be Honest with Yourself	111
10. Be Honest with Your Kids	127

Value V–Exploration

11. Dating, Marriage, and Beyond	149
12. The Joy of Discovery	161

Acknowledgments	175
Appendix I: Discovering Your Cultural Values	177
Appendix II: Resources for You and Your Kids	182
Notes	185

Foreword

When I was a kid, I used to dream of chestnut-colored hair. Growing up in Tokyo, I distinctly remember standing down below the bustle of the city, looking through the crowds at the subway station. I would gaze from head to head—it was a personal game or a whisper I didn't dare say loud enough to hear. Was there anyone here with chestnut brown hair?

My own hair was black as night until I started dying it in college, and then it later began to gray with age. My skin was light brown, and my eyes were light brown too. My dad used to say, "Did you know your eyes were green when you were a baby?" I would always respond the same way, "Green like yours?"

My mom's eyes are raven black, so dark you couldn't distinguish between pupil and her midnight iris.

I was glad my eyes seemed to be right in the middle—a blend of both of them. In my reflection, I saw a dual connection, and it made me feel like home. I wished my hair did the same thing and would pray it to be so that I didn't have as much explaining to do for my existence.

My existence: a Mixed-race girl. It was never considered normal . . . only wrong or too special to be understood. In Korea, my Mixed existence was responded to with teenage spit and words I won't repeat here. In midwestern high schools, strangers responded with questions, assumptions, and an oppressive curiosity.

As an adult, I learned about history I wasn't taught in school—there were laws in our nation that sought to prevent Mixed-race people from existing. Learning about anti-miscegenation laws was sobering, and it also helped me understand why I had always felt such resistance, subtle or outright, to living a life of embrace for my whole story.

My parents, a Korean immigrant mother, and a Californian white father, loved me whole, and my experience at home was one that affirmed our reality. What we were was normal. It wasn't until I went out into the world and began to face the reality of our American history, world history, biases, and worldview of others around me that I began to reckon with the question, "Who am I?"

I've spent years since then answering, unpacking, processing, and rejecting those questions. What I needed all those years ago, and what my family needed, beyond, "I love you just the way you are," was the ability to name our reality and see how history impacted our reality in the world.

These days, I am a mother to Mixed-race kids and aware that this group of people is the fastest growing group in our nation. More than ever before, our American families and faith communities need language, stories, and those who can guide them in understanding and embracing Mixed-race identities. We don't just need one story about our experiences, we need many for our growing demographic, just like the many colorful stories that most of us embody.

Nicole's book does just that, and Nicole is a wise expert and guide for any family who has a member who is Mixed. Reading the stories, data, and helpful tips she's complied are a breath of fresh air. Her compassion and honesty are what we need as we consider the generations to come and what it will mean to serve, see, and love them well.

We are not a little bit of this and that; we are whole humans. We are no longer a mere side note to the American experience; we are the future face of our nation.

Tasha Jun
Author of Tell Me the Dream Again: Reflections on Family, Ethnicity, and the Sacred Work of Belonging

Introduction

I am biracial, Christian woman: all weighty descriptors. I am glad to be a woman, and I am glad to be a Christian. My faith has always brought me joy, stability, and peace. I don't always understand God, but he has anchored my soul like no one else could. Without God, I no doubt would be a hapless wanderer. Being biracial is another story. For decades, I wanted to shed my skin, like a molting snake, and emerge something different, something less confusing. I didn't like the ambiguity *biracial* brings with it but wished I could plant my feet firmly in one world or another. Now, finally, after a long circuitous journey, I feel at home in my skin; *biracial* feels like a blessing rather than a curse, intentional rather than random, something to be embraced and enjoyed rather than spurned and denied. My wish is that your kids will discover this level of stability and self-acceptance much sooner than I did.

Sometimes the thing that causes us the most pain becomes a well from which others can drink. For me, being biracial was the source of tremendous angst. We simply cannot be happy when we don't know who we are or when we don't like who we are. It has taken longer than it should have for me to be at peace in my skin.

My goal and hope in writing this book is to provide insight for interracial couples who have or who are planning to have children. I'm also writing to parents who have adopted children of another race and single parents. Parents who adopt transracially, even if those children are monoracial, will likely also find many insights applicable to their multiracial families. You chose to clear the hurdles of racism and create a family. Love triumphed, and that truly is a beautiful thing. Doubtless your kids are or will be surrounded by love, but the fact that you picked up this book means that you know at least on a subliminal level that raising strong, grounded, happy kids in a multiracial family requires more than love.

I am biracial, Black and white, so my story comes from that perspective, but this book is written for parents of all biracial or multiracial kids: Black and Asian; white and Asian; indigenous, Black and Hispanic. The possibilities are almost endless, and I include stories from families of various identities as well. I trust that you'll be able to take the ideas shared and apply them to your unique family.

I am also a Christian, and I want to speak for a moment to those readers who are not Christians. Because my faith in God has been so central to my life, it comes up a lot. I'm not including Scriptures to try to convert you or preach at you but rather to try to explain where I'm coming from and to be as true to myself as possible. You don't have to be a Christian to gain insight from the values I offer. The principles shared are important for anyone with a multiracial family, regardless of religion. I'm glad you're here! I'm glad you're reading!

A word about my parents: they were/are extraordinary (my father is deceased, my mother lives not far from me). They were smart, present, and kind. I was loved, cared for, and given broad, rich experiences. I wasn't a joyful kid, but my childhood was not tragic by any means, and some of my malaise would have been there no matter what my parents did. Some of us are born with a level of melancholy that we simply have to manage ourselves. When it came to raising biracial kids, my parents did what they knew to do. There were so few resources back then,

INTRODUCTION 3

so few books, articles, or friends with like experiences, so little transparency, and, of course, no internet. When I talk about the things that I wish they did, my purpose isn't to throw them under the bus but rather to identify some things that may have made a difference in my life so that you can help your kids love the skin they are wrapped in *before* they reach adulthood.

I also want this for my own children. They are Mixed racially and culturally. My husband immigrated from Jamaica as a young adult, and though I often think of my kids as Black, they do have a white grandmother whom they regularly see. We also live in a very white suburb in a very white school district, and perhaps because of my own childhood malaise, I am very aware that they could subconsciously resent the skin that makes them feel so *other* so much of the time. I write this book both as a parent endeavoring to raise grounded multiracial kids and as an adult child of parents who could have benefited from more guidance raising children to love and embrace every part of themselves.

Race in America is deep and primal. In the last four centuries, myriad bills have been argued and laws passed dealing with it: Is it legal to harbor escaped slaves? Will enslavers be prosecuted if they kill their slaves? Can Black people become citizens? Can Black men sleep in the same military barracks as white men? Can Black and Brown kids go to school with white kids? Can they swim with white kids? Can BIPOC (Black, Indigenous, and People of Color) men marry white women? Can Japanese Americans be incarcerated in internment camps? The Indian Removal Act, Kansas–Nebraska Act, Chinese Exclusion Act, Civil Rights Act, Three-Fifths Compromise, Missouri Comprise—tomes of legislation about race and ethnicity, all trying to control numbers, integration, and who gets to be considered human—these quandaries have preoccupied American courts for almost four hundred years. It makes sense then that kids who carry within themselves two or more races, each with different histories, one perhaps considered superior to another, would experience angst and would need an extra measure of guidance.

I don't say this to scare you. Your kids will have challenges others don't have, but they will also have opportunities others don't have. God gave you these kids and will give you everything you need to raise them.

When I read through the conversations in various online groups for multiracial people, I see so much hurt and anger over racial identity. They've been told how to identify, and they resent it. They don't feel fully Black or fully Asian or fully Hispanic, yet white people treat them as if they were and monoracial BIPOC shut the door to full acceptance because they aren't. They feel as if they don't fit anywhere, that they're on the outside of life looking in. I felt that way, too, for a long time.

Solomon enjoins us in Proverbs 4:7, "Wisdom is the principal thing; therefore, get wisdom. And in all your getting, get understanding." In the chapters that follow, I will discuss five core values that will help provide some of the wisdom you need to raise happy Mixed-race kids. Each of these values—awareness, humility, diversity, honesty, and exploration—has its own section. Also, at the end of most chapters you will find questions to ponder and steps for application, according to the ages of your children. The steps are not meant to be prescriptive. You can't and shouldn't do all of them. Rather, see them as a bucket of suggestions for you to find the ones that feel most useful for your family. What strikes a chord, provides confirmation, fits with your personality and circumstances? They're meant to get the juices flowing, not to tell you what to do. I hope they're helpful.

The journey of raising your amazing kids will not be easy, but it will surely be beautiful, interesting, and full of wonder. I am delighted to be on it with you.

1

What about the Children?

I was a product of my parents' crime.
—Trevor Noah[1]

When my dad proposed to my mom, she didn't say, "Yes." Instead, she uttered the words no suitor wants to hear: "I'll think about it." It was 1962 in Colorado Springs. My dad was stationed at Fort Carson, and my mom had fled to the Springs looking for succor and a fresh start after a failed relationship. They met, dated, and fell in love. The reason for my mom's ambivalence about marriage had everything to do with race: she is white, and my dad, now deceased, was Black. She had grown up in small-town Pennsylvania, where Black folks lived on one side of the tracks and whites on the other. Yet her mother had always taught her that racism was ridiculous, that it made no sense. And so, my mom made Black friends in her integrated schools and then sat with them in the balcony of the segregated movie theater: her first but certainly not her last acts of resistance against a racist culture.

Nevertheless, she was fully aware that falling in love with a Black man was forbidden by most, and that nearly half of the country stubbornly held onto antimiscegenation laws. Interracial marriage was incredibly rare, and my parents' lives would not be easy. It would take another five years, when I was one year old, before the Supreme Court overturned the last of these laws. But in that moment, the dominant question in my mother's mind was, "What about the children?"

My parents spent a lot of their dates at the Black Elks Club (one of the few places they were welcome together). One night, they enjoyed drinks with a friend who happened to be biracial, and my mom asked him what it was like: how did he fare being Mixed race? He replied that he was loved by both his parents, and that's what mattered the most. "If your kids are loved," he said, "they will be all right." My mom knew that love would not be an issue, and so she finally said yes.

But love was not enough.

For most of my life, I felt a two-ness akin to the one W. E. B. Du Bois described: "One ever feels his two-ness—an American, a Negro; two souls, two thoughts, two unreconciled strivings; two warring ideals in one dark body, whose dogged strength alone keeps it from being torn asunder."[2]

My angst was not over being Black and American but rather over being Black and white. I felt fully welcome in neither world and, for a while, I wandered in a no man's land of racelessness: lonely, struggling with self-esteem, feeling the strain of two unreconciled strivings. Striving characterized much of my life and so much of that was because of race. Why can't I be like the Black girls? Why can't I be like the white girls? Full acceptance by my peers felt unattainable, and I rejected the parts of myself that seemed to be the culprit: It's my whiteness! It's my blackness! Perhaps if I closet one, then I'll fit in somewhere. That was not a happy endeavor.

Korean and white author Tasha Jun shares similar feelings: "I've always felt unfit as a Korean but somehow too Korean everywhere else."[3] And writer Alia Joy so poignantly states, "I felt God had somehow made me wrong. I wasn't fully white and I wasn't fully Asian. Two halves of something that didn't seem to add up to a whole."[4]

Such feelings are not unusual among Mixed-race people. In 2020, Vox conducted a survey of Mixed Americans and noted,

WHAT ABOUT THE CHILDREN?

Over and over again, we heard from respondents that they frequently felt isolated, confused about their identity, and frustrated when others attempted to dole them out into specific boxes.[5]

If you are the parent of Mixed-race kids, you can help to mitigate this loneliness and identity confusion by intentionally teaching your children to love the way they were made. But how? Even though the Mixed-race population is the fastest growing demographic, few resources exist to help parents raise these beautiful kids. Psychologist Sarah Gaither dedicated her graduate work to fill in some of the gaps. She confirmed that more than "mono-racials," multiracial people have to answer the question, "What are you?" "This can lead to feelings of identity crisis and social isolation, especially if in answering the question people feel they have to choose between their parents."[6]

And yet, she also held out hope, reporting that if biracial kids are raised to identify with both parents and to understand their complex racial heritage, they can have higher self-esteem than monoracial people. "They are adaptable [and] able to function well in both majority and minority environments." Not only that, but they are more likely to reject the lie of racism.[7]

How powerful! Dear parents, this is the wonderful job before you: to raise Mixed-race kids who identify with both of you, who love all parts of their cultural heritage, who know that God made them beautifully, wonderfully complex and that this is an asset, not a liability. The purpose of this book is to come alongside you and give you tools and encouragement to help you on this fantastic journey.

All parents need wisdom, a realistic view of the world, and an extra measure of good judgment, especially when their kids are different, a different race from their peers, or a different race from either or both of their parents. These kids are swimming upstream. They are pioneers. All parents need acumen but how much more when your child is singular?

One white friend who is a parent of biracial kids acknowledged, "My experience is not going to be their experience.

I need to be humble and listen." This is so apt. So many monoracial parents of multiracial kids don't consider that their children will have a completely different experience than they had growing up. Parents, you are in new territory. Listen to your kids; if you have a partner, talk to each other about your experiences related to race and learn from each other. You both bring such good stuff to the table, and your kids will need it all.

QUESTIONS TO PONDER

1. What anxieties about parenting multiracial children did you have before becoming a parent? Do you think you had a realistic understanding of what their experience might be like? Why or why not?

2. Have you ever wondered if, since your kids look Asian, or Black, or Hispanic, you should just raise them to identify that way? For example, "Since Isaiah looks Black, we're going to raise him to be Black since that's how others will see him anyway." What might be the value of raising your child to identify as biracial or multiracial regardless of his or her dominant features? Is there a downside to this?

3. What was your racial experience like growing up? Was race an issue in your childhood? How do you think your child's experiences will be different from your own? Does this make you nervous?

4. What kinds of conversations have you had with your child's other parent about racial identity development?

2

Color Matters

[My mother] wanted me to understand there were two sides to me, and she didn't want me to feel like I had to pick one or one was better than the other. . . . She said, "Your father is a Russian Jew. This is his background. And I want you to be proud of that. And . . . we are of African descent by way of the Bahamas. And that is your culture and that is beautiful as well. And I want you to accept that, but society is only going to see you as Black. They're not going to see the other side."

—Lenny Kravitz[1]

God knit us together in our mother's womb, and we are marvelous to behold. The same is true for our children. God determined their skin tone, their hair texture, the shape of their nose, whether they would have a petite, athletic body or a round, curvy one. I know all about genes, but God created genes, and he can mix them and manifest them anyway he chooses.

During much of my childhood and adolescence, I didn't like the way I looked. I hated my hair, and the way it frizzed up in the rain or on humid days (which is every day in the summer in Brooklyn). I hated what happened to it when I emerged from the water at the beach; within seconds it went from sleek, to curly, to a frizzy mass of tangles. I wanted it to stay sleek like white girls' hair. I also didn't like the way my light brown skin made me feel *different, other,* like I didn't belong with my Black peers, and I didn't belong with my white peers either.

And then one day a friend looked at me and said, "You know you're beautiful, right?" I thought she was joking, but then she challenged me to read Psalm 139, and though I had read it many times before, it was as if scales fell from my eyes: *Oh yes, you shaped me first inside, then out; you formed me in my mother's womb.... Body and soul, I am marvelously made!* (vv. 13–14 *MSG*).

That Scripture catalyzed my journey to self-acceptance.

Your kid is God's kid. She is loved unconditionally and created to do amazing things that only she can do. She possesses gifts and tendencies and a personality molded by the Divine. God breathed life into her, and she is exceptional, unique, one of a kind. Kids do best when they know they are accountable to someone and when they know they are loved unconditionally. I tell my sons all the time, "God is there, even when we're not, watching you and loving you. So live right! And don't be dismayed if friends reject you. The One who created you will never reject you."

They still do dumb things sometimes, and they still feel sad when a friend pulls away, but my hope is that this mantra will become part of their subconscious and will help to mold them into secure, grounded men.

Our children, however, aren't spiritual beings, floating through life without a body. They have a body, and that body has a color, and that is both wonderful and consequential. Those passing them on the street or sitting in the boss's seat on the other side of the desk or wearing the uniform when they are stopped for going a little too fast will see first your child's color, and other ethnic details, even before they see their gender. That's just the way it is, and there's nothing we can do about it.

This is not, in and of itself, bad. One of the things God decided when he formed us in the secret place was the slant of our eyes, the curl of our hair, the quantity of melanin in our skin. A couple can have three Mixed-race kids with completely different physical traits. One may be very fair, another possessing ebony skin, and another a soft mocha complexion. One may have cascading light brown hair and another dark, tight curls. God ordained it all. All of it is beautiful, and all of it has a purpose. There is no good hair or bad hair: no such thing as too dark or too light; no good eyes or bad eyes. God crafted all of it, and those whose ancestry springs from Norway will be lighter than those whose forefathers were taken from Nigeria. God determined our origins and our physical traits, and God declared all of it *good*. Norwegians and Nigerians carry equal amounts of God's image. Japanese and Jamaicans are equally amazing.

Tasha Jun writes, "(T)hese gifts of ethnicity and culture are love letters from God. They are deliberate tools that reflect his love and intention." I love that: *deliberate tools*. Our ethnic heritage is not accidental; it is not unfortunate or shameful. We don't have to pretend it doesn't exist, and we don't have to assimilate into some sort of colorless, featureless mass.

Color blindness is an insult to the One who created color. Color should be seen, embraced, and appreciated, never denied or scorned. The question isn't whether people will see your child's color; of course they will! The question is, will he be treated differently if he has darker skin? Will he be afforded the same level of dignity as someone with a much lighter complexion? His physical features will be part of his story, and your role is to help him craft a strong, confident narrative, especially since the world will try continually to reshape it.

As a parent of multiracial children, you have the privilege and joy of teaching your children to see and appreciate all of themselves, including their color. Jun writes about her journey of self-acceptance: "I began to realize that I couldn't know God's love for me unless I accepted and uncovered all of who he has made me to be."[3] Your kids need to be able to look at themselves fully in the mirror and know that God created all that they see. He didn't make any mistakes; it is all beautiful, all lovely. They also need to know the richness of the cultures commingling in their veins.

Defining Terms

Before we discuss the first of the five values I mentioned earlier, let's define some terms. It's good to make sure we're on the same page before we proceed much further.

race: Categories based on skin color and other physical features.

ethnicity: The culture of people from a geographic region, including their language, heritage, religion, and customs.

biracial: People whose parents are two different races. For example, Black and white, white and Chinese, or Black and Filipino.

Mixed-race: People whose parents are two or more races.

multicultural: People whose parents may or may not be the same race, but they have different cultures. For example, African American and West Indian, Italian and German, or Chinese and Canadian.

Black: People whose parents both descended from Africa.

white: People whose parents both descended from Europe.

BIPOC: An acronym for "Black, Indigenous, People of Color." Anyone who is not white.

racism: The belief in a racial hierarchy.

white supremacy: The belief that white people and white culture are superior to nonwhite people and culture and that they dwell at the top of the hierarchy.

QUESTIONS TO PONDER

1. Have you ever thought that color blindness is a good thing, that your kids' Christian identity or their human identity is the only truly important part of their identity? If so, what makes you hesitant to highlight racial differences?

2. Have you ever worried about whether your kids will be treated differently because of their color or ethnic features? How do you think you can prepare them for this possibility?

3. Do you ever talk to your kids about their features? Have you told them that their skin, their eyes, their hair are all beautiful? How have you sought to reinforce this truth, for example, with the art on your walls, the magazines on your coffee table, the picture books you read to them?

4. Are any of the terms in the list above new to you? Are any of the definitions surprising to you?

16 WHAT ABOUT THE CHILDREN?

STEPS FOR APPLICATION

Toddlers and Preschoolers

— Read picture books featuring diverse kids and talk about how lovely they all are. If you are Jewish or Christian, read Psalm 139 to your little ones. Lay it on thick that God made them just right: their hair, skin, eyes, nose, and mouth are perfect and beautiful.

Elementary School

— Teach your kids that their skin is brown, for example, because Dad's great-great-great grandparents came from Africa and Mom's greats came from England. And that they are a wonderful combination of both! Help your kids to understand and appreciate why they look the way they do.

Tweens and Teens

— Provide books about the grandeur of past kingdoms in Africa, Asia, or Latin America, wherever each side of their family is from. Don't depend on school to instill this pride in your kids.

VALUE I

Awareness

3

Race, the One-Drop Rule,
and Cultural Racism

> Identity in America for biracial people has been complicated. Racism has played a major role in this complication. . . . Some people want you to feel guilty for being mixed and identifying as biracial, nothing else. This group supports biracial identity. We are mixed! I will not apologize for being who I am! There are biracial selections on the census, job applications, medical documents, dating websites, and even driving tickets. It's time we put an end to the "one drop" ideology. We are biracial and multiracial people. Love us or hate us, we will NOT change!
> —Biracial in America Facebook group description[1]

Awareness is the first value we will discuss. Since you have children who are Mixed-race or have adopted children of another race, it's important for you to know where the idea of race came from, the subtleties of racism, and why historically Mixed-race people have had to choose one race over another.

Many years ago, a white college friend queried, "Why can't you just be a person? Why does figuring out your race matter so much?" I wish those who had constructed the idea of race in the first place had considered this. I wish those who segregated our country based on melanin content realized the absurdity of it all. But from the very beginning of our nation's history, race has been a "thing," and the strict boundary between white and nonwhite observed at all costs.

The Invention of Race

One of the first to suggest racial categorization was German scientist Johann Blumenbach. His theory proposed that there are five distinct races: Caucasian, Mongolian, Malayan, American

Red, and Ethiopian. He based these categorizations on skull size and shape, and he considered the Caucasian skull the most beautiful.[2] Later, skin color, hair texture, eye shape, and nose width were added to the formula to determine race and worth. Caucasians were placed at the top of the pyramid, said to possess the most intelligence, the most attractive features, and the greatest value, and everyone else was stratified underneath. Indeed, some considered nonwhite races an entirely different and inferior species.

Race theory crossed the Atlantic at a very opportune time. In eighteenth-century America, when some were beginning to criticize the inhumane trafficking of African people, race theory provided a solution to salve the gnawing conscience. If African men were subhuman, created only to serve, then it was perfectly fine to shackle them. If African women were not really women, then selling their children was little more than selling the foals of a horse. Indeed, enslaved Black women were routinely called *mares*. Similarly, if Native Americans were just savages, taking their land was reasonable and just; savages wouldn't know how to steward such lush land anyway. If you want to steal land or steal labor, you just have to convince yourself that they are both rightfully yours.

David Hume, a Scottish philosopher, boldly declared. "I am apt to suspect all Negroes, and in general all other species of men . . . to be naturally inferior to the white."[3] There you have it: "species of men." The idea that there are different species of men, some better than others, lay at the root of the deep racial division we still experience today.

One Puritan judge said in 1700, "To prove that all men have equal right to liberty, and all outward comforts of this life . . . [is] to invert the Order that God hath set in the World, who hath ordained different degrees and orders of men, some to be High and Honorable, some to be Low and Despicable . . . yeah, some to be born Slaves, and so to remain during their lives."[4]

Similarly, Cotton Mather, son of Harvard University's first president, said, "The state of the Negroes in the world must be low, and mean, and abject, a state of servitude, no great things

RACE, THE ONE-DROP RULE, AND CULTURAL RACISM   21

in this world, can be done for them. Something then, let there be done, towards their welfare in the world to come."[5] Many believed that it was in the Africans' best interest to be enslaved by the white man and then converted to Christianity so that they might receive salvation, even if on this earth they were bound to menial labor.

One Southern philosopher noted, "If there are sordid, servile, and laborious offices to be performed is it not better that there should be sordid, servile, and laborious beings to perform them?"[6] Latinx and Asians were also at various times in U.S. history considered laborious beings.

When the United States won the Mexican-American War in 1848, the Treaty of Guadalupe Hidalgo granted the United States 55 percent of Mexican territory and with that territory thousands of Mexicans who were granted American citizenship. This was good news for the Southern Pacific Railroad, which wanted cheap labor. But Mexican Americans were never really treated like citizens; they were forced into barrios and their children denied access to good schools. By the 1920s, fears about them taking all the jobs grew to such an extent that two million people were forcefully deported, the vast majority of whom were already American citizens.[7]

Asian immigrants have a similar story. Around the time of the Civil War, the United States welcomed Chinese laborers to help build the transcontinental railroad. These workers were considered inferior to whites but were paid wages for their work. About a decade after the railroad was finished, however, Congress passed the Chinese Exclusion Act, banning any more Chinese from entering the United States. Japanese were demonized in the World War II era, Chinese during the McCarthy era, and Koreans and Vietnamese during the Korean and Vietnam Wars.

Throughout the last 150 years, anti-immigrant hostility has tragically culminated in vigilante violence, including lynchings of men, women, and children. Today, anti-immigrant hostility is on the rise once again, as nativist groups use terms like *aliens* and *Chinese virus*; some are even trying to get birthright citizenship, guaranteed by the Fourteenth Amendment, repealed.

In the United States, capitalism and racism have always worked in tandem. We import or invite nonwhite people in service to capitalism, and then we want them to leave because of racism. The underlying assumption is that America is a white nation, and nonwhites can come to serve white people for a time, and then they must leave. Some even hoped that African Americans would return to Africa after emancipation. In 1816, several prominent white men founded the American Colonization Society (ACS) to deal with "the problem" of free Blacks in the United States. The mission of the society was to move liberated Black people to Africa. Members included Henry Clay, Daniel Webster, and John Randolph; Presidents Thomas Jefferson and James Madison also supported this vision. In 1821, a Navy ship found a suitable location, which was later named Liberia, and by 1838, twenty thousand formerly enslaved Black people had crossed the Atlantic and settled there.[8] The truth, however, is that America has never been a white nation. People of color have always been here—even before white people.

Deciding that BIPOC were subhuman provided justification for slavery, servitude, and genocide, all to build the American economy. In other words, race theory was an economic necessity. As historian Ashley Montagu noted, "The idea of race was, in fact, the deliberate creation of an exploiting class seeking to maintain and defend its privileges against what was profitably regarded as an inferior social caste."[9] This racial caste system still exists today. A Harvard study suggests the persistent entrenchment of America's racial hierarchy, which assigns the highest status to whites, followed by Asians, then Latinx and Blacks at the bottom.[10] White supremacy is part of America's root system that has never been extracted.

The One-Drop Rule

The sharp distinctions between races that white supremacy demanded were complicated by the reality of Mixed children, some of whom had very light skin. With supposedly essential racial lines blurred, it was harder to know how to classify someone. Because of rape, and the rare occasion when mixed-race couples actually fell in love, rules had to be established to deal with Mixed offspring. Maryland passed the first antimiscegenation law in 1664. Other colonies followed, and interracial marriage remained a criminal offense in most states for almost three hundred years.

The One-Drop Rule of 1920 legally assigned minority status to Mixed-race individuals. Now if you had just "one drop" of Black blood, for example, you were considered Black.[11] You could not be white *and* Black; you had to be white *or* Black, and you were Black if you possessed any African feature or if anyone knew you had any Black relative. The same was true for those with Asian, Indigenous, or any other nonwhite heritage.

In Louisiana, even as late as 1983, "anyone whose ancestry was more than one-thirty-second Black was categorized as Black"[12] and in 1985, someone with a Black great-great-great-great-grandmother (i.e., one sixty-fourth Black) was barred from identifying as "white" on her passport.[13]

Several years ago, the hullabaloo over the British royal family's alleged racism was all over the news. They knew Meghan Markle, Prince Harry's bride, was biracial, but she looked white and so was allowed through the hallowed doors. But what about their children? Genes can be capricious. You can be completely light skinned, with a narrow British nose, and give birth to a dark baby with fuzzy hair. What if Meghan and Harry produce a Black baby? How could a Black baby be a royal? In the minds of some, the one-drop rule lives on.[14]

Whiteness was defined—and "protected"—by exclusion and separation, and those who dared to jump over the hurdles of separation threatened the dissolution of a well-established social caste system. In the United States, enforcing this caste system meant BIPOC were separated and sequestered away from white people. Those who enforced segregation in the Jim Crow South specifically warned against "race mixing," arguing that Black men would surely rape white women if they were near them. (They failed to acknowledge that, for centuries, it was white men who raped Black women.) There were legally sanctioned white schools, white neighborhoods, white water fountains, white subdivisions, white libraries, white swimming pools, white social clubs, white unions, white churches, white colleges, white art exhibits, white theaters, white restaurants, and white hospitals. If a city couldn't afford a separate structure, then they just established times when white and nonwhite people could use it separately. For example, only once a week in some cities could Black people use the library, and only from certain sections could they check out books. In Chicago, Black people could swim in the public pool only on Wednesday nights; they could never swim at the same time as whites as Black people were considered dirty, diseased, and lascivious, unable to control themselves around white women in bathing suits.

It's true that some Europeans who immigrated in the late nineteenth and early twentieth centuries, like Jews, Italians, and the Irish, were barred from certain amenities, too, but for a much shorter time. Soon, these ethnic groups were enfolded into whiteness and afforded humanity. They were allowed to intermarry, obtain skilled jobs, and hold positions of power and authority as in police and fire departments. They could buy homes in most neighborhoods, and their children could attend white-only schools. At a time when Puerto Ricans were redlined into slums and when Blacks faced clubs and dogs for trying to vote, an Irish Catholic was elected President of the United States.

Clearly, even the European Americans who faced the most discrimination were never treated the way nonwhite populations were treated. Native Americans were killed or pushed onto reservations, Mexican Americans forced back to Mexico or into barrios, Chinese pushed into Chinatowns, and Blacks into inner-city slums. Black and Brown neighborhoods all over the country offered only tenement housing, substandard schools, negligible health care, and terrible working conditions. By the 1940s, some 80 percent of Latinx children in California attended separate schools. They were turned away from newer, more beautiful white schools and sent to learn in shacks. School officials believed that Latinx kids, like Black kids, were dirty and infected with disease.[15]

Cultural Racism

Even though legal segregation ended over fifty years ago, we still need to talk about how to help our Mixed-race children love themselves because racism is still so rife in our society. We see the obvious manifestations of it in racial slurs or hate crimes, but there are myriad more covert examples of racism that affect our kids in subtle but real ways. Dr. Beverly Tatum writes about something called *cultural racism*, that is, the "cultural images and messages that affirm the assumed superiority of Whites and the assumed inferiority of people of color."[16] She says this is so pervasive it is like smog in the air. You breathe it in without knowing it. The only way to counterbalance its effects is to breathe in the clean air of truth: that all people are created equal, endowed by their Creator with certain inalienable rights. You breathe in clean air by reading about the contributions people of color have made. You reject the mere suggestion of genetic superiority, knowing we are all part of the *imago Dei*, equally sinful, equally loved, equally special. And you seek to discover why disparity exists, refusing simplistic, smug answers to difficult problems.

You don't have to look far to see cultural racism in the things we look at and listen to.

I remember watching a television police series with one of my sons. After seeing about six or seven episodes over the course of a couple of weeks, I asked him, "Hey, what color are the bad guys—usually?"

He responded, "Um, Black or Hispanic."

"Yes, and what crime are they usually committing?"

"Um, they're usually drug dealers."

When I told him the majority of illegal drug users and dealers in America are white, he looked at me in astonishment. *Really?!* It saddened me that my son subconsciously believed that people who looked like him were mostly responsible for the drug trade in America.

In the media, Black men are over-represented as perpetrators of crime, and Black suspects are presented as more threatening. Black mug shots are shown more often than white, and the perpetrator's color is more often mentioned on the radio if he is Black.[17] All of these things reinforce the Myth of the Dangerous Black Man, which has existed since Europeans first set foot on the African shores.

Hollywood presents Blacks and Hispanics as dangerous gang members or welfare recipients. Hispanics are gardeners or maids, rarely doctors, lawyers, or judges. Asian men are daft and powerless or brutal and emotionless. Asian women are cute or oversexualized.

The Myth of the Model Minority is a subset of cultural racism that also negatively affects Asians. The myth states that Asians are polite and successful and that their success is due to hard work plus innate intelligence. Asian kids are math whizzes, Asian women are tiger moms, and Asian men work in STEM. And all the while, Asians are relegated to the position of permanent foreigner. The myth does damage in several ways. First, it makes Asians into a monolith; it doesn't take into account that Asia is the largest continent on the planet, including not only China, Korea, and Japan but also India, Burma, the Middle East, and more. In America, some Asian immigrants have graduate degrees and high-paying jobs, but many do not. Yet the myth states that because of hard work and not getting caught up in talk of racism, all Asians have achieved the American Dream. The myth strips Asians of their individuality and pushes them all onto the poster of American meritocracy. Asian children can't fail. Asian employees can't grieve. Asian women can't have a bad day. Asian men can't feel. Trying to live up to superhuman standards is a contributing factor of the high suicide rate among Asian college students. They have the typical immigrant/minority pressure to achieve, plus this myth to live up to.

The myth also pits Asians against other BIPOC who may have lower achievement rates. *Why can't you be like the Asians?* gets hurled at other people of color and creates division among those who would otherwise find comradery in each other. Asians also get rewarded with white approval for staying quiet about racism, where those who don't are branded troublemakers, race baiters, and dividers.

Whether you're trying to protect your child from the Myth of the Dangerous Black Man, or the Myth of the Model Minority, or any other racist myth out there, you are your child's trusted guide through their childhood years, and you are the first line of defense. You are the one who can see, evaluate, and battle back the long-term toxic mold of cultural racism.

Likewise, you can combat racist myths and assumptions with information. Do your kids know why racial disparity exists? Kids notice that many suburban areas are mostly white and that most inner cities are mostly BIPOC. They see the difference; don't ignore it and pretend it doesn't exist. They see the disparity, and if we don't teach them why it exists, they will likely draw false conclusions that will inflate or deflate their self-esteem.

Does your child know why so few Asians inhabit leadership positions, why Asian women are objectified and Asian people, including the elderly, were targeted during the COVID-19 pandemic? Does he know that these things happen because of ignorance, hatred, and racism, not because there's something wrong with Asians? Does your child understand where Asian stereotypes come from and why they are false?

Does your child understand why there's such a dramatic wealth gap between white and Black people in America? White Americans hold ten times more total wealth than Black Americans.[18] Hispanics have a little more wealth than Blacks, but nothing close to that of whites. But why? Either white people really are superior, working harder, and making better choices—or systemic racism really does exist. Either BIPOC have had the same opportunities but can't take advantage of them because of genetic inferiority or people have been systematically denied opportunities to make wealth. In other words, either white supremacy is true or systemic racism is true. Which do you believe, and which will you teach your kids? Neither science nor Scripture indicates genetic superiority. Rather, it is a lie created to divide and oppress people.

I remember sitting at the dinner table and telling my boys that in the Unite States, there are more poor white people than poor Black people, and they were both so surprised! What we see on TV or in certain sections of the city is Black and Brown poverty, so they assumed that Black and Brown poverty was greater. I explained to them that poor whites tend to live spread out in rural areas, while poor Black and Brown people tend to be clustered together in inner cities, and whenever poverty is concentrated, it is both easier to see and also compounded in its effects. I've told them that poverty breeds certain ills and wealth breeds certain ills and though we want to be careful about ranking sin, the Bible speaks more about the sins of the wealthy than the sins of the poor. Poverty is never presented in Scripture as a moral failing, rather Jesus says, "*Blessed are the poor!*"

We teach our boys why our city, Rochester, New York, is so segregated and why the suburban schools are so white. The difference in quality between the city and suburban schools does not mean that white people are better but rather that the city was intentionally segregated and the consequences of that are vast and far reaching. We make sure that they know that despite so much hardship, the majority of Black and Brown people have left poverty behind.

Dear parents, white supremacy is part of America's root system, so much so that in most art and in most movies, even Jesus has been depicted as a white man. It is absurd to suggest that a Middle Eastern man would have white skin, but white supremacy rejected the idea that Jesus could possibly be Brown and demanded that he have white skin, flowing blond hair, and blue eyes. This alone kept some Black people from becoming Christians. It was a stumbling block set in place by a racist culture. How tragic! Yet how wonderful that there has always been a remnant church who rightly believed that white, Black, or Brown, all people bear his image, and not the other way around.

Even people of color can believe that white is better; after centuries of seeing racist images, being treated with contempt, and held at arm's length, it can be difficult to believe in your own equality and worth. We owe it to our children to uproot any trace of white supremacy from our lives and intentionally teach them that white is *not* better, no matter what the wider culture tries to tell them.

I'm reminded of an experiment conducted in the 1940s by psychologists Kenneth and Mamie Clark called the "Doll Studies." They used it to demonstrate the negative effects of segregation on Black children: segregation gave children a sense of inferiority that stayed with them for the rest of their lives.[19] This test is often repeated to this day, and sadly the results are the same. A group of Black and Brown kids is shown a white baby doll and a Black baby doll, and then asked a series of questions: *Which one of these dolls is the mean doll? Which one of these is the bad doll? Which one is the ugly doll?* After each of the above questions, Black and Brown kids all pointed to the brown doll. They were then asked: *Which is the skin color adults like the most?* Now, for the first time, each child pointed to the white doll. On the last question, *Which doll is your favorite?*, all the girls chose the white doll. When asked why, they said, *"because the white doll has prettier eyes (blue)."*[20]

The test was even given in Singapore to Asian kids, this time with a white doll, a light brown doll, and a dark brown doll. The kids responded in the same way; they all preferred the lightest doll.[21] All of these BIPOC kids have breathed in the smog of cultural racism their whole little lives and now subliminally believed that the doll that looked the most like them was mean, bad, and ugly, and they also believed that adults prefer those who look the least like them. Parents, please do what it takes to protect your kids from this kind of heartbreaking self-rejection. Let them know that their skin, light, dark, or somewhere in between, is beautiful.

QUESTIONS TO PONDER

1. How many famous nonwhite people do you and your kids know about? What kinds of contributions to our society did they make? Do your kids know about BIPOC scientists, authors, and leaders, as well as athletes and musicians?

2. Why do you think the average white family has more wealth than the average Black or Brown family? Why do you think Black and Hispanic men are incarcerated at a disproportionally high rate? If you don't know, seek out reliable information.

3. What examples of cultural racism do you see? Think about the television shows you watch or news media you consume.

4. Has the Myth of the Dangerous Black Man or the Myth of the Model Minority negatively affected you at any point of your life? How?

5. How often are your children surrounded by BIPOC people from races and ethnicities that are not represented in their own backgrounds? Do they feel comfortable in those situations? Do they know that Asian, Hispanic, or Black culture is dynamic, multifaceted, and beautiful, not static or monolithic?

RACE, THE ONE-DROP RULE, AND CULTURAL RACISM   31

STEPS FOR APPLICATION

Toddlers and Preschoolers

—Realize that by age two or three, children start to develop racial biases,[22] but you can help your little kids by building their strong foundation of God's love for them and God's love for others.

—Buy diverse dolls and action figures. Note, they may initially want only white dolls, like their white friends have, and you can certainly provide some white dolls, but most of your children's toys should resemble them. You can say something like, "Sally has white dolls because she is white and she wanted dolls that look like her, and you are Brown, so we are giving you dolls that look like you. Your Brown dolls are just as pretty and just as special as Sally's white dolls."

Elementary School

—At birthdays and holidays, especially holidays related to their culture, gift your children with books featuring Black and Brown people who've made important contributions to our country and world.

—Explain racism, white supremacy, prejudice, and other terms in a way that your kids understand and that reflects God's perspective. Use phrases like "God made everyone with equal value no matter our color or culture," "Racism is wrong, but loving everyone like God does is right," and "You are precious to God inside and out." Reinforce these phrases by writing them on note cards to post on the refrigerator or bathroom mirror or to place on the dinner table for discussion. This will help embed these valuable truths into their young minds.

32 WHAT ABOUT THE CHILDREN?

—Little eyes are watching! Your kids will passively notice whom you invite over to your home, so be intentional about your friends and acquaintances. Pay attention to those comments that you make about delivery drivers or other visitors to make sure that you are consistent with what you are teaching them.

—Open your front door to diversity! Invite diverse kids over for playdates and encourage your child to invite new diverse friends over too. Brainstorm with your kids about how to invite diverse families over once a month or once a quarter for dinner. Be sure to create a warm, welcoming atmosphere and remind your family to be generous listeners. Don't forget to ask the family if there's anything they don't like to eat, as different cultures may have different food restrictions.

—Try various ethnic restaurants so that your kids get used to different tastes, smells, and decor. Discourage your kids from sticking with the familiar. Let them know that it's fun to try new foods. They will sense your enthusiasm; if you're excited about something new and different, they will be also.

Tweens and Teens

—Listen with your ears and heart! Kids tell us things all the time, but we have to stop and listen. As your kids talk about social media, notice what they are watching and talk about cultural racism. Ask questions like, "Do you agree with that influencer?" or "If you were to make that video, what would you say instead?"

—Open their eyes. If you're watching an episode of a show that shows racial bias, ask your kids if they saw racial bias and what stereotypes were reinforced, such as *Black people are criminals* or *Caucasians work harder.* You can ask questions like, "Why do you think that character was written to be that color?" or "What types of stereotypes is that character reinforcing?"

— Pre-watch movies and documentaries about racial bias, the wealth gap, and injustice and then ask your kids to watch with you. Ask questions like, "What seemed fair to you or unfair for the people of color?" or "Where do you see things getting better or worse?" or "What do you have control over or no control over in your life?" Give your kids a chance to process circumstances that will become their adult realities, but reinforce hope, God's help, and their own opportunity to make a difference.

4

Colorism

I've heard some Black people say, "Well, mixed people aren't actually Black." . . . I would also hear things like, "Oh, well, it's a shame that Thelma is not more light-skinned." It's like, I'm not Black enough, but I'm simultaneously too Black.
—Thelma, Black and Chicana.[1]

As long as there has been a United States of America, there have been mixed-race Americans.
—Ronald R. Sundstrom[2]

If your children have a range of color tones, they need to know that they are all equally loved and accepted by God and by you, and any positive or negative bias they experience from others does not reflect on them. By teaching them this, you are providing a shield, a forcefield, against inferiority or superiority. Ignoring the reality of colorism won't help them. Your kids need to know that it exists, and that it is a lie.

If you are not familiar with the term *colorism*, it's a subtle subset of racism that will impact your Mixed children in one form or another. It is a cultural pecking order that rewards lighter-skinned people over darker-skinned people, and it is the natural outgrowth of white supremacy: the closer one is to whiteness, the more privilege one receives. While our culture's failure to eliminate racism continues to wound people of color, the wound deepens when colorism sparks division and infighting among Black and Brown people themselves. People may think your lighter daughter is more attractive than your darker daughter. Police may find your darker son more suspicious looking than your lighter son. Teachers may assume your lighter child will achieve higher grades than your darker child. It stinks. It's terrible, but it's reality.

Skin color is a spectrum, and the closer someone is to the light end of the spectrum, the more beautiful she is considered and the more privileges she gets. All over Asia, Latin America, Africa, and the African diaspora, colorism has divided people of color. Many darker people resent the better jobs, the better treatment, the more noble assumptions lighter-skinned people so often receive. They know they are more palatable to the culture at large, and some view them as sellouts. Some assume they feel superior, and I am sure there are lighter-skinned BIPOC who do feel superior. But even if they do not, many face suspicion and resentment from their darker peers.

I know someone with a light-skinned daughter and a dark-skinned son. Her daughter is considered beautiful, and her son is considered dangerous. She gets positive attention, and he gets negative attention. He notices this and resents it. The mom is now trying to find counseling for her son to get over his anger and learn how to deal with racism in a healthier way. She chides herself for not seeing this sooner and dealing with it proactively. Don't let your kids be hit broadside; prepare them and buttress them by constantly telling them how lovely they truly are.

In 2005, *Glamour* magazine interviewed the adult children of Black R&B musician Quincy Jones. He and his white wife had two daughters: one light, the other dark. "While Kidada spoke of identifying as Black—as everyone perceives her to be—lighter Rashida elaborated: 'I had no control over how I looked! This is my natural hair; these are my natural eyes! I've never tried to be anything I'm not. Today I feel guilty, knowing that because of the way our genes tumbled out, Kidada had to go through pain I didn't have to endure.'"[3]

People will react to your child differently based on how light or dark he is. If you have a light-skinned baby, people may wonder if he will *darken up*. Black people may use expressions like "bright" or "high yellow" when they see your lighter child. Sometimes they are saying these things as compliments and sometimes not. If your lighter daughter has longer, straighter hair, some may remark, "Oh, she's got the good hair!" Others may comment that your darker child should stay out of the sun.

In W. Kamau Bell's documentary *1000% Me*, a Mixed Filipino and white woman shared that her Filipino family told her to stay out of the sun so that she wouldn't become too dark: "No one will marry you if you're dark," they warned.[4] In a survey, 62 percent of Hispanic adults said that having darker skin limits their ability to get ahead. They said that the darker you are, the less intelligent you are perceived to be.[5]

I know someone who is one of ten kids. She said while growing up, the lighter kids were often invited to birthday parties and other gatherings that the darker kids were not. This is extreme, but the wounds from colorism can be deep. You won't be able to completely shield your children from it, but you can mitigate its effects.

Sometimes it's not just about color but also about features. Kids who are partially Asian, for example, may have very light complexions but may vary in terms of features, and those with more European attributes may have an easier time dodging racism. Whether it's about skin color or other physical traits, the message from our wider culture is the same: the whiter the better.

While this may all feel unfair and daunting, there are proactive measures you can implement to inoculate, protect, and prepare your child for the impact of colorism. We'll get there soon, but first, I want to give a brief history of colorism because to combat it, you should know where it came from.

The Origin of Colorism

As we discussed, race theory ascribed the highest value to those of European descent: those with the lightest skin and the most European features. This is the essence of white supremacy, and colorism is the natural outgrowth of white supremacy. The closer one is to white, the better one is treated. Because Europe conquered or colonized most of the world, white supremacy and colorism pollute most places on earth.

In America, colorism among Black people began during slavery when lighter-skinned slaves received better treatment and special privileges that darker slaves could not access. As a result, the darker slaves often resented their lighter-skinned co-laborers and rejected them from their community. These lighter slaves were fathered by their enslavers, who had undeterred freedom to rape enslaved women as often as they wanted. It was the perfect way to increase the labor force and assert domination over the women as well as over their fathers, brothers, and husbands who could do nothing to stop it.

These Black women were voiceless, the Black men were voiceless, and the enslavers' wives were nearly voiceless. The white wife may not have had the power to stop her husband's nocturnal exploits, but she did have the power to unleash her bitter resentment on the slaves. She could target and torment the slave child and his mother. She could suggest the sale of one or both if money were short or if she just couldn't stand having them around. In other words, her voice was revenge.

There was a time when plantations teemed with these light brown children, and as they grew, despite the ire of the white wives, they often received special treatment from their fathers. They were spared the hard, sweltering field life and given easier tasks inside: cooking, cleaning, and caring for the master's white children, their half siblings. The practice of giving lighter slaves easier work encouraged colorism: a pecking order and division among Black people. Resentment and suspicion flourished under these conditions, and that resentment and suspicion linger to this day.

These light-skinned offspring were called *mulattos*, that is, *mules*: half horse and half donkey. Today most biracial people reject this label and choose to be called *biracial* or *Mixed-race* instead.

It is noteworthy that the first novel published by an African American was titled *Clotel*. In it, William Wells Brown relates the story of a biracial woman named Currer and her two "quadroon" daughters, Clotel and Althesa. Brown wrote the novel in 1853 to expose the complex trials of Mixed-race women on slave plantations. It was quite controversial at the time because Currer was the fictitious paramour of President Thomas Jefferson.

Colorism among other people of color is also deep, pervasive, and harmful.

In Asia, *lighter* has been synonymous with *better* since ancient times. The poor and working class, darker from working in the sun, were considered inferior to much paler wealthy elites who worked inside. Light skin meant wealth and success. "In Asia, there is a deeply rooted cultural notion that associates dark skin with poverty and working in the fields, whereas pale skin reflects a more comfortable life out of the sun and, therefore, a higher socioeconomic status."[6] We can see this sentiment in the Song of Solomon, "Do not stare at me because I am dark, for the sun has tanned me. My mother's sons were angry with me; they made me caretaker of the vineyards" (1:6 NASB). The Shulammite woman is ashamed of her dark complexion and explains that it wasn't her fault; her brothers forced her to work outside in the vineyards.

As Europe conquered and colorized most of the world, the concept that lighter is better went deeper than class. Europeans brought white supremacy with them. Now, rich or poor, those with lighter skin were simply considered better than those with darker skin. This mentality is still deeply entrenched today, and the lighter you are, the more opportunities you have.

So, too, in Latinx communities lighter is also often preferred. "In every Dominican family, because you have such a melting pot of Spaniard, African and Taino origins, you always have a rainbow of colors," says writer Anyiné Galván-Rodríguez. But as a child, she noticed that her physical features determined how she was treated. "While some grandchildren were praised for their looser curls, I was chastised for my coarse curly hair."[7] Because of internalized white supremacy, many Hispanics want to look more Spanish (European) and less African or Indigenous.

Sometimes Hispanics wish for lighter skin simply because they know lighter skin will make their lives easier. In a survey conducted by Pew Research, 62 percent of Hispanic adults said that having a darker skin color hurts Hispanics' ability to get ahead in the United States today at least a little. Darker Hispanics consistently reported that they were treated as if they were not smart.[8]

Thanks to colorism, the dangerous practice of skin bleaching, which chemically reduces the amount of melanin in the skin, is a multibillion-dollar industry targeting women of color all over the world. Advertisements in Asia and Africa portray women getting their dream job or their dream husband by making their skin lighter. Similarly, many Black men and women have tried to make their hair as straight as possible, first with hot irons and hot combs and then with chemical relaxers. We've all seen those pictures of James Brown, Al Sharpton, back in the day, and even Malcolm X before he converted to the Nation. I remember a white stylist suggesting that I get my hair straightened before a professional photoshoot. She thought I'd look better. Now, plenty of Black women still relax their hair and there's nothing wrong with that, but there is something wrong if straight hair is considered more beautiful and more professional than natural hair.

The point is Black men and women should be allowed to wear their hair anyway they like. Legislators have sought to pass a federal law called Creating a Respectful and Open World for Natural Hair (CROWN) Act, but it has been delayed, so some states have passed their own version. It protects Black people from discrimination if they happen to wear locs, braids, twists, or knots. Sadly, this is necessary because athletes have been kicked off teams, kids embarrassed by teachers, and employees fired, all for wearing Black hairstyles instead of white hairstyles.

Preparing and Protecting Your Child

So how do you protect your children from colorism? First, pay attention. As a simple test, do an online search for the most popular African American or Latinx celebrities. Note the skin tone of these men and women. What do you see? Beyoncé, Jennifer Lopez, Michael B. Jordan, Regé-Jean Page, Halle Berry, Mariah Carey—all of these are light, and they are considered the most beautiful, handsome, and noteworthy. Darker actresses, like Viola Davis and Simone Ashley, the dark-skinned Indian actress in *Bridgerton*, all have commented about how much harder it is to get significant roles in Hollywood when you happen to have more melanin in your skin. Even Bollywood reveals a consistent preference for lighter-skinned Indian actors and actresses.

In movies and TV shows, lighter-skinned BIPOC women are often the *exotic* beauties pursued by the most handsome men. They have big eyes, moderately plump lips, and moderately round hips. Their skin mocha and never too dark, their hair flows long and sleek, never kinky or textured. They are enchanting, mysterious, exotic, *different*—but not *too* different. They check all the diversity boxes without shocking anyone.

My dear readers, remember that *awareness* is our first value, and being aware of colorism is crucial so that you can be proactive and intentional. Celebrate the color of your children's skin during every stage of life. Comment about the beauty of your lighter kids and the beauty of your darker kids. Let them know that God thought about their skin, planned it, delighted in it. Whether there's a lot of melanin or a little, their skin is beautiful and perfect and good. Let your darker daughter know that she is stunning and brilliant. Let your darker son know that he was knit together in your womb perfectly and his rich, gorgeous skin is a delight. Help your kids to find shades of clothes and makeup that look great on their skin; teach them to proudly wear bold colors. Not everyone can wear orange and yellow well, but they probably can, and should!

Remind them, often, that assigning greater value to those with less melanin is both random and ridiculous. Ground them in the truth that melanin content has nothing to do with beauty, intelligence, or virtue and intentionally point out examples of dark, beautiful people.

Biracial NFL player Colin Kaepernick shared his experience with colorism in his Netflix miniseries *Black and White*.[9] In high school, most Black boys sought to date white girls, but Kaepernick liked a dark-skinned Black girl, labeled "blue black" by his peers; she was undesirable to everyone but him. To the shock of his friends, he asked her to the school dance. To him, she was beautiful, but when he brought home the picture of them together, his adoptive white parents looked at it with disdain and hid it away in a drawer. She was just too dark. He went to the next dance with a white girl, and that picture his parents framed and placed on their center wall with pride. The second date was considered lovely, stunning, a prize. Proximity to whiteness equaled proximity to beauty, with white women being considered the most beautiful of all.

My dark-skinned sister-in-law, Michelle, ruminated about colorism in Jamaica, a Black nation rife with colorism left in the wake of British rule. Growing up, Michelle's dark family had a light-skinned Jamaican maid who often said to her, "I'm going out to get you some white skin!" Each time, Michelle felt excited; finally, she would have lighter skin. Disappointment always followed when the maid returned home empty-handed. I wonder if this lighter maid was trying to assert her alleged superiority, even as she served this darker family.

When the census takers came to her house, and her mother checked her as *Black*, Michelle cried out in despair and begged to be checked *Indian* instead. As she grew, she felt unattractive when men, attempting to have lighter children, chose lighter women. Thankfully, a male friend told her that she was just as beautiful as those women. And, indeed, Michelle is now happily married to her very dark husband.

For decades, lighter-skinned Jamaicans won every beauty pageant. In television ads, lighter Jamaicans sold beauty products, where dark women sold laundry soap. Light-skinned people received better jobs and higher wages and worked in more visible positions as companies assumed that customers seeing lighter skin would increase sales. One dark man who owns a high-end jewelry store very intentionally hired a light-skinned woman to be the "face" of the store as he knew wealthy customers would be more likely to make a purchase from her than from him.

Rastafarianism, however, brought significant, positive change to Jamaica. Rastafarians are pro-Black, and to them, a dark Black woman is an empress, a queen, worthy, valuable. You can see this change of mindset within music. Buju Banton's song "Love Me Browning" once dominated:

> Me love me car Me love me bike
> Me love me money and ting
> But most of all, Me love me browning[10]

Browning is slang for a light-skinned woman. However, when there was a public outcry against this song, Banton released "Love Black Woman," which praises dark-skinned women. Now when DJs choose "Love Me Browning," they immediately play "Love Black Woman" right after. And in 2017, Davina Bennett, with an unapologetic afro and dark brown skin, became Miss Universe Jamaica.

In an attempt to counteract society's obsession with physical appearance, some parents deemphasize it and shy away from complimenting their kids on their looks, but historically, darker people have been made to feel ugly or less attractive than lighter people, so it's important that our children know that not only are they good, but they are also beautiful. Of course we should emphasize character, but thanks to racism and colorism, we also need to lay it on thick that, light or dark, our kids are gorgeous.

In 2022, *The Root* published a discussion comparing actresses Keke Palmer and Zendaya. Both started their careers as children, and some argue that they are equally talented, but Palmer is less known to mainstream audiences than Zendaya. Zendaya is biracial with light skin and has had an easier time navigating Hollywood.

She acknowledges her privilege saying, "Being a light-skinned woman, you know, to recognize my privilege in that sense as well and make sure that I'm not taking up space where I don't need to. . . . I am Hollywood's acceptable version of a Black girl and that has to change."[11]

Nurture this kind of self-awareness and honesty in your children. They need to know whether they are benefiting from colorism or being diminished by it. If your lighter kids know that they are partially BIPOC, and if they take pride in the BIPOC part of them, if they embrace it, not to the exclusion of their whiteness, but in addition to it, darker people around them will sense comradery rather than superiority. It's as if your child is saying to darker peers, "I know I am lighter, and will have some privileges you don't, but I don't feel superior to you. I know that if a racist finds out I have a BIPOC parent, I might be treated poorly, too, so we're in this together. I am with you in standing against racism. I'm not ashamed of my heritage; as a matter of fact, I'm proud of it, all of it!" (I remember the day a man in a truck honked at me and yelled "N-word" through the open window. He didn't care that I was lighter, just that I was brown.)

Your children obviously won't say this to every BIPOC person they meet, but if this attitude is in their hearts, it will emanate and manifest in their words and attitudes. Darker people will sense it and feel harmony, rather than hostility.

If your child is partly Asian or partly Hispanic, their features will likely be different from someone who is fully Asian or fully Hispanic. They may even pass for white, but do they know they are not fully white? Do they know how to relate to and gain the trust of someone who looks more Asian or Hispanic than they do? If your kids are around positive Asian or Hispanic people often enough, they will understand that culture and feel proud to be part of it, and this pride will emanate from things they say and do.

QUESTIONS TO PONDER

1. Where have you seen examples of colorism?

2. Do your kids have a range of skin tones? Do people treat your lighter ones differently from your darker ones? How does this affect their relationship with one another?

3. Have your darker kids or kids with more ethnic features ever expressed dismay over their hair, eyes, skin? How have you tried to build their self-esteem?

4. Do your kids gravitate to those with lighter skin or more Eurocentric features? Whom do they consider handsome or beautiful? Who are their favorite actors and actresses?

5. Do you feel more threatened by dark-skinned men than lighter-skinned men? If so, what can you do to ameliorate this bias? How can you prepare your dark-skinned son for this kind of cultural bias?

WHAT ABOUT THE CHILDREN?

STEPS FOR APPLICATION

Toddlers and Preschoolers

—Notice the language that you use within your household as well as the language your extended family uses to describe your children. While you can't control what others say, you can request that adults highlight character qualities as well as their physical traits and that they do so equally for all your children. For example, you can say, "Can we talk about not only how handsome Jevon is but also how well he is learning to tie his shoes or what good hugs he gives? I want him to know that his character is really important too. And when handing out compliments, be sure not to leave out [darker] DaMien! He's super handsome too!

Elementary School

—When watching movies or television with your children, point out the names of actors of color of every shade, with all kinds of ethnic features. Knowing their names will increase familiarity. Try to do a quick online search to find out unique facts about their lives to help your child remember them beyond being famous.

—When watching movies or animated television shows, pay attention to any hidden bias. You can ask your kids questions like, "Did you notice any difference in how the lighter-skinned or darker-skinned characters were treated?" If you notice color bias, ask, "How was the lighter-skinned character treated differently?" followed by, "How should we see everyone, no matter their skin shade?"

COLORISM 47

—Listen to their words. Pay attention when washing your child's face or combing their hair. They will often reveal little wounds from words spoken on the playground or by a family member about their skin color. If they express something negative about their appearance, stop and listen, and then tell them the truth of their beauty and worth.

Tweens and Teens

—Educate them. Use the content from this chapter to teach your children about the origins of colorism. It's helpful to be as honest as you can about what happened during slavery and how colorism pitted lighter slaves versus darker slaves. Ask your children about how that would have made each set of slaves feel and whether they've felt colorism impact their lives. Or talk to them about how Europeans brought white supremacy with them when they colonized the globe. Talk to them about its damage in Africa, Asia, and Latin America, and even though these regions won their independence decades ago, the lie that whiter is better still damages people there in myriad ways.

—Though you'll need to explain the realities of colorism in our culture, balance that out with God's truth about them. Remind them often of the *imago Dei*, that they were created in God's image and that he does all things well. Also remind them that though their skin is beautiful, they are so much more than their skin.

VALUE II

Humility

5

Cultural Shibboleths Matter

"My mother understood very well that she was raising two black daughters. She knew that her adopted homeland would see Maya and me as black girls, and she was determined to make sure we would grow into confident, proud black women."

—Kamala Harris[1]

Jephthah captured the shallow crossings of the Jordan River, and whenever a fugitive from Ephraim tried to go back across, the men of Gilead would challenge him. "Are you a member of the tribe of Ephraim?" they would ask. If the man said, "No, I'm not," they would tell him to say "Shibboleth." If he was from Ephraim, he would say "Sibboleth," because people from Ephraim cannot pronounce the word correctly. Then they would take him and kill him at the shallow crossings of the Jordan. In all, 42,000 Ephraimites were killed at that time.

—Judges 12:5–6 NLT

Humility is the second value we will discuss: humility to learn and appreciate the cultural values of your spouse and his or her extended family and then to intentionally teach these values to your children.

In the Bible passage above, the men of Gilead established a test to determine belonging. They needed a way to identify their enemy, the Ephraimites, and so as they stood guard at the Jordan River, if someone tried to cross, he would have to say the word *Shibboleth*. If he dropped the *h* and said *Sibboleth*, the men of Gilead would know he was an Ephraimite, and they would kill him. This was a test of identity and belonging, and not belonging had deadly consequences.

The word has come to mean, more generally, a word or custom that distinguishes one group from another. Every group has shibboleths. The wealthy members of a country club check to see the kind of car you drive to make sure you really belong. Board members check your academic credentials to make sure you're really up to snuff. Cliques at school have ways to determine if you're really one of them; are you cool enough, fast enough, smart enough?

Shibboleths are based on values, and the above examples reveal social values: money, academic prestige, coolness. But cultures have shibboleths, too, and though you may reject some of them, many are important for your children to know and appreciate. These can include things like music; hair and clothing styles; language; food; slang; attitudes toward time, money, and authority; expressiveness; politeness; and more. It takes humility to learn, understand, and embrace values that are different from your own, but part of raising grounded Mixed-race kids means knowing the cultural values of your child's other parent and making room for them to be passed on to your kids.

Kristina, who is Filipino and white, writes, "In college, friends would take me to Filipino student group meetings, and I just always felt like an imposter, like I didn't have a right to be there."[2]

You can help mitigate this imposter syndrome by partnering with your spouse to teach the shibboleths or values of both sides of your kids' cultural heritage. If you feel as if your ways are superior or you simply want your children to assimilate into majority American culture, your kids will grow up one-sided, and that will hinder positive identity formation.

The Problem with Not Knowing Shibboleths

Shortly after my parents married, my father was honorably discharged from the army, and they moved from military to civilian housing. They thought they'd stay and raise a family in Colorado, but two things forced their hand to move. First, my father could not find a job, other than menial labor. It was still true in much of the country that a Black man could serve in the military, willing to die for his country, but still be denied a skilled job in the civilian sector. And second, they began to receive death threats.

One day, my mom, visibly pregnant with my sister, went to the mailbox and retrieved a letter with a newspaper clipping. The clipping detailed the death of a woman who had been locked in a closet and her house set on fire. The accompanying message read, "This is what will happen to you and your [N-word] family if you don't leave." Since the letter had been sent through the United States Postal Service, the FBI investigated and assured her that such threats rarely lead to anything. Still, my father dusted off his Army-issued sidearm and tried in vain to teach my mom how to shoot. She hated pulling the trigger and failed to hit the target every time. It was a lost cause. Fear sullied their newly married lives, and double-checking the locks on the door became a nightly routine. Shortly after my sister was born, my parents decided to leave Colorado for good and move to New York City, which is where I was born.

My birthplace had everything to do with race.

My parents found a large, rent-controlled apartment in a diverse community in Brooklyn, and Brooklyn, of course, is adjacent to Queens, which is the most diverse city in the world. Our apartment building housed Latin Americans, African Americans, some white hippies, and us. I remember the Panamanian family downstairs: the dad and teenage sons, proudly washing and waxing their car every Saturday morning, music blaring from the radio as they worked. The African American family with a single mom and her seven kids. She sang at her church, and her voice filled the courtyard when she practiced nearly every day. The superintendent's family who got to live there for free since he carried the load of fixing the myriad things that went wrong in that Victorian-era building. I remember another Black family with five kids; their mom occasionally watched me after school until my mom returned from work. These were hardworking families with firm discipline. The mothers clipped branches from the large oak tree out front to use as switches to keep their kids in line. Disrespect was forbidden.

You would think this would have been the perfect place to grow up and learn about my Mixed heritage, and in some ways it was. I went to school with kids from buildings like ours and kids from elegant brownstones. Rather than sending their kids to private schools, most wealthy white parents decided to integrate the public schools. They used their time, education, and influence to make sure all kids got a quality education, and everyone benefited from the economic, racial, and ethnic diversity in our schools. (Sadly, my neighborhood has now been gentrified. My apartment building has been turned into million-dollar condominiums and families like mine could never afford to live there. I'm sure the working class has retreated to lower income areas and the schools are likely much less diverse.)

Even though I grew up in such a culturally rich atmosphere, I still struggled with identity confusion because I didn't understand Black shibboleths. My mother didn't recognize the need to know them, and my dad was uninvolved. As a result, when I was around my Black peers, I constantly felt like I was being tested and that I was always failing. This compounded a sense of *otherness* and resulted in a loneliness that marked my childhood.

One shibboleth which eluded me was carefully groomed hair. Hair was a test determined by my peers to gage blackness, and I failed it.

Like so many white women with Black and Brown children, my mom didn't really understand our hair. She didn't understand the need for grease, the need to keep it covered in the rain or secured under a bathing cap at the beach. And she was way too practical to sit for hours, carefully securing tiny little braids with multicolored rubber bands. So, we often just wore two braids separated by a tolerably straight part but surrounded by untamed fuzz.

I didn't understand it then, but I understand now why *hair* is so highly valued by Black people. The first Black millionaire, Madam C. J. Walker, became wealthy at the turn of the twentieth century by creating and selling beauty products first for Black women and then for Black men. At the time, the idea that a Black woman could be beautiful and take pride in her appearance was revolutionary. For centuries, and still in part today, whiteness was the standard of beauty. White hair, white body types, white skin, white features: these made you beautiful, and if you didn't have them, you couldn't be beautiful. Black women were property, maids, nannies: not women who could be feminine or lovely. Beauty and blackness were oxymorons. Walker became wealthy by selling the idea to Black women that they, too, could be pretty, that Black hair and Black skin were worthy of primping. Just like white women, Black women could stand in front of a mirror and be pleased with what they saw.

Taking pride in their appearance, going out in public looking their best, became ways of rejecting the idea of ugliness and inferiority. Black women and Black men could be proud of who they were. They could be beautiful too. Valuing beautiful hair isn't frivolous or silly. It's part of dignity.

Today I see the look of pride on my sons' faces when they return from the Black barbershop freshly coiffed. My husband brings them on this biweekly pilgrimage and there they watch the barber place finishing touches on the customer before them; he pays careful attention to every facial hair: perfect sideburns, perfect edging, a perfect beard. Then that customer leaves with a satisfied smile, and my sons take turns in the chair. At the end, they eagerly snatch the mirror and inspect the perfect work from every angle. They leave, grateful, with a grin and freshly squared shoulders.

It would have been good for me to leave a beauty shop with squared shoulders too.

Is hair a big deal in your child's diverse culture? If it is, do you know how to cut and style it? Can you ask someone to teach you, or rearrange your budget so that you can pay someone to do it? This is not a waste of time or money but rather an important part of identity development.

I have a white friend who has two biracial daughters, and she realized that she didn't have the time or patience to learn how to do their hair, so she and her husband made the financial decision to regularly send them to a Black beauty shop. Her girls have learned to patiently sit for hours as the beautician washes, greases, and braids their hair, and they love the results when she's finally done. I love this example of humility and openness in my friend to understand that her Brown girls need something that she didn't need as a child.

I also failed the second test of blackness: Clothing.

My mom has always been practical and frugal—and my parents had very little discretionary money. What extra money they did have went for piano lessons, dance lessons, summer camp, and summer vacation. My mother wanted us to have extracurricular activities. She also wanted us to appreciate nature, to leave the concrete jungle once a year and enjoy wide open spaces. She saw no need to spend good money on pretty clothes. Therefore, most of our clothes were passed down from friends, and they didn't match.

For Black and Brown people, nice clothes are also part of dignity. Many BIPOC bore the shame of poverty for so many generations that when a family was not poor, it was very important for everyone to know that they had left poverty behind. My paternal grandfather, for example, grew up having no shoes, and by the time he died, he owned over a hundred pair. They were carefully chosen to go with the dozens of suits he wore with pride.

My mother had no such pride. She had grown up working class, and the rationing of the Depression and World War II years left an indelible mark on her; she would ever be parsimonious and careful with money. She also adopted much of the hippie mindset of the time: spurning vanity and materialism, preferring an au naturel look, which was the opposite look of the Black and Hispanic women around us. In this way, my mother's cultural values were at odds with those of the women of color around us. It would have been good for her to acknowledge and respect the culture of the person she married and allow those values to influence and nuance her own. If your spouse or partner does things differently or if their culture in general does something differently, embrace humility, ask questions, seek to understand, and then come to an agreement together about how you're going to raise your kids. Whose values will prevail in your family, or is it possible to elevate both in a way that honors both parts of your children's heritage? Pride says, *my way is the best way,* but humility counters, *both have merit.* How can we teach our kids a combination of each?

Looking back, I appreciate my mom's decision to use most of our extra dollars for piano lessons and reprieve from the city. In the big picture of my life, these would prove very important to me. But I do wish my parents had used a little more money to help me feel pretty so that, like the Black girls around me, I could lift my head with dignity too.

Parents, are there certain styles of clothes or manner of dressing that are important to your child's cultures? It is not unusual for my West Indian husband to send our boys back upstairs to change; to him, there are school clothes, play clothes, and church clothes, and you don't go to school or church in sloppy clothes (and certainly not in pajamas). Does your partner have similar values? Can you find a way to compromise and figure out together how you want your kids to dress in public?

Hispanics and Asians similarly tend to value dignity and personal grooming, and they often dress more formally for work, church, and parties. Spending money on clothes, hair, nails, and shoes is not considered vain to them but is an important part of honor and pride.

The third test of blackness I encountered growing up was athletic ability, and I failed that one too. I ran with a slow, awkward gait. No one wanted me on their team. Playing tag was torture; I knew I'd be tagged first and then agonize trying to tag someone back as the other kids danced around me. I could never catch them, and often I gave up in tears.

And then there was Double Dutch, the ultimate Black girl's pastime. With two left feet and no confidence, there was no way I'd ever master that skill. I'd jump in and get tangled up in the ropes every time. I gave up, and the other girls took over, moving with ease and grace. I just stood there, both resenting them and wishing I could be like them.

Going outside to play felt like entering a hostile world where everyone expected me to fail, and often, I did fail.

Is athleticism an important cultural value for you? We opted for music lessons over sports for our boys, but we also make sure they know how to play basketball at least a little, since hooping is a rite of passage for so many Black boys. We want them to feel comfortable in Black *and* white circles and knowing how to hoop is part of that.

Perhaps playing an instrument is a cultural expectation. For example, many Asian-American kids take private music lessons. Political scientist and author Michael Ahn Paarlberg remembers, "At age 5, I was given a quarter-size violin. Private lessons followed, with regular trips to the Kennedy Center to see the National Symphony Orchestra. By 12, I was concertmaster of my school orchestra and performing solo recitals. . . . At no point did I feel I had much of a choice in the matter." And violinist Sarah Chang said candidly, "Music is a huge part of life for most Asian families. Most Asian children I know start taking violin, piano, or cello lessons from an early age." If this sets them apart socially from their non-Asian classmates, Asian parents largely do not care.[3] Are music lessons very important to your Asian partner? If so, decide together whether you will make this part of your children's lives.

For me, playing classical music was problematic because in my Black peers' minds, classical music was for white people, and because I played it, I was "acting white."

I also liked soul music; I wore out my Ike and Tina Turner and Aretha Franklin albums and sang "Proud Mary" and "Respect" loud and proud. But when someone had a dance party and everyone started to move, once again, my body failed me. I was too self-conscious, and self-consciousness is the ultimate saboteur of dance. How could I loosen up and express myself when *myself* was so unacceptable to all the kids around me?

What musical genres should your kids be familiar with so that they can relate to others within their culture? Are there certain "must-know" dances that you or your partner should teach them so that they don't feel out of place when everyone else from that culture starts to move to the beat? Even though our boys play classical music like I did, they hear reggae, hip-hop, and R&B played on vinyl in our home. We want them to know and appreciate those genres too.

Growing up, I also failed the "School Test." I grew up in the era of tracking, which in my school meant that the bright students landed in Track One, average students in Track Two, and the slower kids in Track Three. I tested into Track One, comprised mostly of white students. So, when the kids from my building saw me hanging out with white kids in school, this was the coup de grâce. I was a traitor to my race: "You think you're white!" they accused. "You think you're better than us!" I didn't think I was better than them. I wanted to be like them, but I couldn't access that.

Some tests are not worth passing. The kids in my building had subconsciously adopted the racist view that Black kids aren't smart, and they accused me of being a sellout because I landed in Track One.

The manner in which people address one another—especially one's elders—can also be a cultural shibboleth. I recall the day, when I was about ten years old, that I committed a nearly unpardonable sin: I addressed one of the Black moms in our apartment building by her first name. "Hi Loretta!" I chirped. She looked at me as if I had spat at her. I still remember her tone, "I am Mrs. Jones." I never made that mistake again, as her dress-down stung for weeks. Over the years I came to understand why so many Black women and men have such a visceral response to disrespect. Mrs. Jones and her husband were part of the Great Migration: Black people who moved up North from the WWI era through the 1970s seeking to escape the South's toxic racism and find better jobs. The Joneses had grown up at a time and in a place where Black people had to glance down and step off the sidewalk to let white people pass; they could expect to be respected by no one but their kin. Honor was a precious commodity, and when these families moved up North, many determined that they would never willingly do without it again.

How should your kids address elders? Even in adulthood, many BIPOC place a *Miss* in front of an older woman's name. For example, most of my Black friends call my mom *Miss Jane*, rather than simply *Jane*. Respecting age or position by using titles or prefixes is valued in many cultures. What about yours?

While we're on the topic of kids interacting with adults, should children freely speak to adults and be part of a conversation or should they be seen and not heard? If you have adult friends over for dinner, can your children actively listen and offer their insights, or should they remain quiet and ask to be excused as soon as they're done eating? How familiar should children be with adults? My husband grew up one way, and I grew up another; we've had to discuss this and find a happy medium. Now that they're teenagers, our kids sit with us when we have friends over, and they can chime in with their thoughts, but they're discouraged from dominating the conversation and encouraged to excuse themselves when they're done eating. We want them to be comfortable around adults and know how to speak up for themselves around teachers, doctors, and others, but we also want them to know that life doesn't revolve around them and when it's time to bow out and let adults enjoy each other's company without them. We're trying to teach them humility *and* confidence.

Some of this speaks to the positive aspect of code-switching. Code-switching is when you change your language, behavior, or clothing depending on the circumstances. Most of us refrain from using slang in professional settings. We unconsciously switch from the more comfortable speech patterns we use around friends and family to standard English at the office. Or we may speak a language other than English at home and then shift to English at work, and there's nothing wrong with that. We want to be understood in professional settings and comfortable when we're at home. We may also wear non-Western clothing for family gatherings but Western clothing at work. Using some sort of vernacular with family and friends or wearing traditional clothing communicates pride, solidarity, and ease.

As parents, one of the things we want to teach our kids is how to read the room and pivot depending on who's there. Our kids need to find common ground and relate to those around them, and knowing certain shibboleths will help them to do this.

There is also a negative side of code-switching, which we will discuss in chapter 7.

The Importance of Humility

Parents, foundational to raising Mixed-race kids is humility: humility to know that your way of doing things isn't the only way and it may not be the best way. When you have Mixed kids, you have an obligation to examine your heart and find any vestige of white supremacy, or Asian supremacy, or any other supremacy and learn the cultural values of your spouse. Together, you can choose which ones to elevate. The white way, or the Black way, or the Korean way isn't always the best way. How wonderful that in your household, you get to raise your kids with the best of both.

Ruminate over the cultural values that are important to you and write them down. It would be helpful if you and your spouse both did this separately and then come together to talk about what you wrote. I talked about hair, clothes, and formality with elders. These can all be summed up in one thing: dignity. Dignity is very important to many BIPOC.

I also mentioned the importance my mother placed on appreciating nature. I have found that hiking, camping, and exploring the woods are things that many white people value, whereas athleticism is something many Black people value.

Other cultural values include food and feasting. In certain communities, weddings go on for days, and Thanksgiving and Christmas dinners could feed an army! Church attendance and strong faith are other cultural values. Right now, in America, Black people have a higher rate of church attendance than any other people group. Many cultures place a high value on education. Often immigrants from poor countries grow up hearing the mantra that education is the way out of poverty, and now they have that same expectation for their kids: get as much education as possible. These cultures also tend to be more involved in their children's choices, from choosing what they wear, to choosing classes in high school, to choosing a college and a college major, and even to choosing a spouse. To them, being a good parent means providing sometimes rigid guidance as long as possible, whereas in other cultures, good parenting means encouraging independence as soon as possible.

Some cultures value happiness, personal fulfillment, free time, and thrift, while others emphasize discipline, family honor, extended family, and generosity. My husband and I decided to prioritize visiting family in Jamaica, even if we couldn't also manage trips to places like Disney World. That was a very intentional choice based on the value of knowing extended family and providing opportunities for our boys to be immersed in that part of their heritage. We've also tried to instill in our sons pride in our family name: that they should act a certain way because they are Doyleys. We want them to know that their behavior does not reflect on them alone. Family honor isn't everything, but it is something.

When do you give, and when do you save? What is your attitude about food: should it be plentiful or sufficient? What about time? Is it rude or socially acceptable to be late? Which is more valuable to you: being honest or being polite? Is speaking loudly and emotively among family, friends, and even colleagues normal, or is speaking softly, less emotionally, and waiting turns better?

I'll mention one last major cultural value here: language. Multiracial people often feel like imposters when they don't know the language of their non-English speaking side. Sometimes immigrants want their children to assimilate into American culture as quickly as possible because they think this will help their children to succeed and will help protect them from racism. They deemphasize their native language and customs and encourage full assimilation. Other parents just don't have time to teach the language because they are working so hard. The problem is that these children often find that they don't fit in anywhere because they're not white but they can't speak the language of their nonwhite friends or family.

Columnist Victoria Rodriguez, a biracial Latina who doesn't speak Spanish, writes,

My immigrant father was rarely home from working long hours and travel, so I never got a chance to learn Spanish. And because of that, I have always felt like a fake Latina . . . like I've been in cultural limbo—never belonging to either side. This loneliness was all consuming.[4]

So many biracial people live in a cultural limbo: they don't fully fit into the white world, and because they don't know the language or customs of their minority culture, they're rejected there too.

You may not even know how to readily articulate what you value. You grew up a certain way and never thought about it before, and that is perfectly normal! It has been said that culture is like an iceberg, only 10 percent of it is visible and the other 90 percent is hidden below the surface. Now that you have kids who represent at least two cultures, however, it is important to take some time for introspection and identify some of the hidden 90 percent so that you can pass both sides to your kids. Take your time and discuss these things with your spouse and then work together to intentionally teach the values you both hold dear.

In Appendix I, I offer a resource for helping you identify your cultural values—just to help get the juices flowing!

QUESTIONS TO PONDER

1. How have you sought to teach your cultural values to your kids?

2. Do you think the values of some cultures are better or more in line with Christian principles? For example, some cultures value being future oriented and planning ahead. People from these cultures may emphasize certain verses like those in Proverbs about the ant preparing for winter. By contrast, others who embrace and find joy living in the present highlight Scriptures like Luke 12:24, which encourages us to look at the birds of the air who do not store food, yet God provides for them. Which one is the Christian value? Is it possible that each culture holds a piece of the puzzle, that just as humans individually bear God's image, different cultures reflect different aspects of God's character?

3. Do you think there is such a thing as "American" values (or British values, or the values of wherever you live) that are distinct from any one racial or ethnic culture? Is there value to teaching children how to assimilate to the majority? How do you weigh your own values against those of the majority?

4. Who teaches most of the values in your home? Does this lead to an imbalance in whose values are taught?

CULTURAL SHIBBOLETHS MATTER

STEPS FOR APPLICATION

Toddlers and Preschoolers

— While your children are still young, talk to your spouse, extended family, and other parents about cultural values, such as hair styling, ear piercing, activities, music, and formality with elders.

— Determine which values are tied to cultural history and which are an expression of popular culture. (For example, sometimes clothing styles, like baggy pants, are more an expression of pop culture than a widely established cultural value.) Then you can consider what is important to you and how to honor these values and pass them to your children.

— Sing lullabies in your language to your little ones. Teach them some words, even if you know only a few yourself. Consider learning the language together!

Elementary School

— Reflect. Does your child seem to naturally connect with their diverse culture or with the majority culture? Think through your child's major influences at home, school, or church.

— Observe. If your child attends a school with other BIPOC kids, pay attention to any statements your child makes about belonging or not belonging to their diverse group. If they don't feel as if they belong, ask questions like "What are the differences that you can see?" or "What do your friends do that you don't do?"

— Support. If your child feels rejected by peers who share one part of their culture, keep reinforcing God's love for them and your family values. Also, help them to find nonwhite friends who like them for who they are.

—Adapt. If you notice that your child leans more toward one culture and they are rejected by their other culture, look for ways to learn and adopt some of that culture's values. For example, should you find someone to style their hair, or play different music in your home, or shop at different stores for their clothes? Are there legends and stories they can learn from their grandmother, or books you can read to help them relate to all parts of their heritage?

Tweens and Teens

—Belonging is important. The pressure to fit in is significant in middle and high school. Continue to reinforce your child's worth and your family values, even if they don't enthusiastically participate or respond.

—If your BIPOC kids live in a mostly white school district, they may feel considerable pressure to assimilate to feel as if they belong. They may not admit that, so you can ask about their favorite online influencers, movie stars, and their clothing choices to determine where they are trying to fit in. Look for clubs like Black Student Union, Asian, or Mosaic clubs where they can find belonging with kids who share some of the values of both sides of their heritage.

—Hopefully by now, your kids are proud of the way they look; help maintain that by regularly providing spaces where there are other kids who look like them.

6

You Can't Do It Alone!

The eye cannot say to the hand, "I have no need of you," nor
again the head to the feet, "I have no need of you."
—1 Corinthians 12:21

As iron sharpens iron,
   so a friend sharpens a friend.
—Proverbs 27:17 NLT

The poet John Donne wrote centuries ago, "No man [or
woman] is an island, entire of itself."[1] He was speaking about
human interconnectedness and mutual dependence. We need
one another. This is even more true when two or more cultures
come together to create a family.

As parents of Mixed-race children, learn from each other.
Give each other room to teach, guide, and impart cultural
nuances. Sometimes when people marry, they let the chips fall
where they may in terms of teaching culture, and the parent
with the loudest voice, the greatest influence, wins and instills
the most. But in Mixed families the stakes are too high. If
one parent dominates, the kids will likely grow up lopsided,
only appreciating or understanding one side of themselves. In
many families, it is the mother who takes up the mantle of
teaching culture, and the father takes a backseat role. But
in Mixed-race families, neither can afford to remain in the
backseat. Both parents have to drive. The kids carry within
their bodies two (or more) cultures, and they need both of you
to love and appreciate all of them.

A white friend who has a Black husband and a biracial teenager told me how important it has been to lean on her husband and his experiences, to let him take the lead in teaching about race and racism, and also to be open to hearing from him when she gets it wrong.

If you are a single parent, though, don't worry! Just consider who can mentor you in these areas. If possible, rely on your child's other parent to teach about his or her culture and model those cultural values, and also seek insight from BIPOC extended family and friends. Your biracial child should not be the only person of color in your life.

My mother intentionally provided cultural experiences. She took us to the ballet, symphony, and opera, and she also made an effort to expose us to some Black culture. I remember seeing dancer/choreographer Alvin Ailey and *The Wiz*, but it would have been even better if my father had been involved. Sitting and watching these things with my white mom was good, but it would have been more poignant to watch them with my dad: to hear him explain things, to watch him enjoy these and other cultural expressions. But like a lot of men of that generation, my dad left most of the teaching to my mom.

When I started taking piano lessons and gravitating to classical music, I wish my dad had encouraged me to make jazz part of my repertoire. It also would have been great if he provided me with books by Black authors and taught me about the incredible resilience of my ancestors. My Black forefathers built empires, survived the Middle Passage, sang through their sorrow, taught themselves to read, and refused despair. Despite so much hardship, Black people have produced some of the most impressive minds this country has known. Learning this would have helped me to be proud of the Black in me.

Kids learn about society's dominant culture by default in school; school curricula are rife with white heroes, white authors, and white contributions. Kids, however, learn very little about BIPOC cultures and heroes in school. I can count on one hand (and even have fingers left over) the number of noteworthy Black people my children have studied and the number of books by Black authors they have read in school. The same is true for Asian and Hispanic authors and heroes. So, we parents need to find ways to fill in the gaps. Discover books you can buy, movies you can watch, cultural art exhibits you can go to, and music you can enjoy as a family.

It was only a few years ago that my husband and I fully recognized that our sons are growing up in a multicultural home: white, African American, and Jamaican. In our boys' baby and toddler years, we were exhausted from sleepless nights and consumed with other aspects of child development—like potty training! I did all the cooking and chose all the books. I also did most of the transporting during the week and usually played classical music in the car. At the end of the day, Marvin's "job" usually was to help our sons burn energy before bedtime. He'd take them for bike rides or to the park, but he didn't intentionally teach them cultural things. We failed to grasp the importance of grounding our kids in their ethnic identity, mostly because they were small and we were tired! And then one day we realized that they knew Chopin but not Bob Marley. We were inadvertently falling into the same patterns as my family of origin, with one parent dominating the transmission of culture.

Our kids enjoyed Jamaican food at Grandma's house or when we occasionally got takeout, but that was not enough to fully appreciate it and develop a taste for all the rich flavors. Going to Jamaica for a week or two every other year was not sufficient for them to fully appreciate this part of their heritage. We realized that if we wanted our boys to understand and value it, my husband had to teach it to them. I can buy books, but I can't fully, genuinely teach them Jamaican values and the beautiful nuances of that culture.

And so, Marvin started playing reggae in the car on the way to church on Sunday mornings and cooking Jamaican food most Saturdays. Food is a big deal for Jamaicans, and my boys love watching him cook fish or goat or oxtail on Saturday afternoons; they are his official taste testers. Sometimes we invite friends over to enjoy it too. Marvin is teaching our boys generosity;

there should always be plenty, and it should always be good. You may not be able to give someone money, but you can always give them food. Food is a love language in Jamaica, and my boys speak that language now too.

I tend to be time conscious, always on a schedule. I naturally, subconsciously place limits on how much time I spend on the phone, how long I linger with a friend over lunch, how often I'll stay up late with guests. I am conscious about how much time I will give to a task; I have an internal clock and an internal schedule. I would never just spontaneously pop over to somebody's house, and I would struggle if someone stopped by my house, unplanned, because I always have a plan for the day. Marvin would not struggle, and just by being who he is, he is teaching our boys the largess of putting people before agenda. He's teaching them to go with the flow more, loosen up, and be more adaptable. If plan A fails, no big deal; be creative and think of plan B. Don't be devastated just because things didn't go according to plan. There's always another plan! He is teaching them the resilience of flexibility.

My husband has an astounding work ethic, but after hours or on vacation, he naturally slips into a more laid-back mode: less scheduled, more spontaneous, more intuitive. He doesn't like to plan weekends. He would rather wake up and see what the day holds: What does he feel like doing? Early on in our marriage, I struggled with this; I wanted to know the plan for Saturday. But we've rubbed off on each other, and our boys are experiencing both flexibility and time conscious-ness on a subliminal level. I embrace the process of learning these cultural nuances because I don't think my ways are superior to his. They both have merit. The extreme of either is problematic, and so we influence each other and make each other better. If I had assumed my ways were superior, shut Marvin down, and demanded that we do things like I did, our boys would lack Marvin's imprint and the beauty of the culture that helped to shape him. I am delighted our boys are growing up experiencing both. Your kids should experience both, whatever both may be.

Marvin also regales our sons with stories of the Maroons in his father's line. The Maroons were enslaved Africans in Jamaica who refused to remain in bondage. They escaped and formed their own communities within the interior of the island. They were fierce and proud, and very dark because they eluded white rape. My boys have heard the story of the heroine, Nanny, many times. She led the Maroons in a revolt against the British, and the British were so overwhelmed that they granted the Maroons five hundred acres of their own land, where they went on to thrive in freedom. It was called New Nanny Town, and it still exists to this day.

My boys are proud to have Maroon blood flowing through their veins. When one of our sons was little, he needed to have painful dental work done, and he strengthened himself by saying, "I have to be brave; I've got Maroon in me!"

Maintaining close ties with extended family is also important. When we make our biannual pilgrimage to Jamaica to visit family, our boys bask in palpable love and learn anew how to sift through the patois to understand their grandparents, uncles, and aunts. They experience a Black world and sense the relief of being in the majority. They are proud of their Jamaican heritage. To them, it makes them special, not inferior.

I experienced some of this growing up, too, when we visited my paternal grandparents. I felt loved and seen, and I learned many important, intangible things from them.

My grandparents lived in a huge public housing project in Queens where my grandfather worked first as a janitor and then as a superintendent. He had fought in World War II, but like most Black veterans, upon returning home, he could secure only menial work. The benefits of the GI Bill eluded most Black men. By the 1960s, he was finally promoted to building superintendent, and that gave my grandparents the ability to buy nice clothes, take regular pilgrimages to Atlantic City, and treat us girls to some things my parents couldn't afford.

Sometimes my sister and I would spend a weekend with them, and when we arrived, the first thing my grandmother did was wash our sneakers and dry them on the windowsill; they had to be clean. Then, she'd tackle our hair. We'd sit down between her knees, and she'd comb, pull, grease, and braid for hours. It was a painstaking process, but we emerged freshly coiffed with tiny braids and pink, green, and yellow barrettes. Then we'd try on the latest things she had sewn for us: new outfits, perfectly pressed and matching. Only after that could we go downstairs and play in the playground attached to the building. My grandmother didn't want to give anyone a reason to treat us badly.

I remember my grandmother's hands: strong from years of working as a maid. I remember the large pots of delicious food, the *Jet* magazines on the coffee table, and the plastic-covered couches. When my parents were there, they would haggle for hours over politics or current culture, and I'd listen in on their conversations, taking in names like Jesse Jackson and Andrew Young, Hank Aaron, Sidney Poitier, and Sammy Davis Jr. I loved visiting them, and I felt at home in their world.

When are your children surrounded by their BIPOC culture or cultures? Do they get to rest in the love of both sides of their family? Do they sit and hear legends and stories about their ancestors? Are they familiar with the languages or the thick accents of their relatives?

Culture is defined as "the characteristics and knowledge of a particular group of people, encompassing language, religion, cuisine, social habits, music and arts."[2] Your kids will automatically learn about the majority culture, and both parents plus their grandparents, aunts, uncles, and cousins will help instill their BIPOC culture in them.

I realize this is not always possible. Your kids may not live with both parents. If this is the case, do they see their other parent on a regular basis? Is it possible to talk about how to transmit her cultural values when she spends time with the kids? What about the extended family on that side? Can your kids regularly see those grandparents, aunts, and uncles to learn things you can't teach? How can your kids regularly be immersed in that part of their culture? What about your friends, neighborhood, church community, and school district? Though you may no longer be with your former spouse or partner, your kids still carry within them the heritage of that person, and they need to understand it and be proud of it.

I realize sometimes it's not financially feasible to visit extended family, and sometimes extended family is toxic. Maybe they're just not good influences on your kids. Or maybe you don't have much extended family. Both of my parents were only children, so I had no aunts, uncles, or cousins. Added to that, my maternal grandparents died young, so our only extended family was our paternal grandparents. We had a tiny family that included only three Black people. For this reason, it would have been so good for my parents to curate relationships with other Black people, which we'll discuss more in part 3.

A Note to Adoptive Parents

I've spoken a lot about the importance of relying on your BIPOC spouse and his extended family to instill pride in your children's heritage. But what if you are both white and your kids are BIPOC?

For you, diverse community is critical. So much is being written by transracial adoptees about the turmoil they experienced growing up in all white communities with parents who didn't think about race or provide any scaffolding for them to navigate race and racism. I'm thinking of Rebecca Carroll, a biracial author who was adopted by a white couple and raised in rural New Hampshire. She writes, "To be adopted into a white family that did not see or care or think about my blackness or my experience navigating a racist country had always felt lonely and isolating, endlessly confusing, but now [as an adult] it just felt cruel."[3] Or Kathryn D'Angelo's words about raising her adopted Black son, "Given the science on the experience of exclusion, we knew we needed to find communities where the psychological desire to connect with like provides him an easier path to belonging. That necessitated finding spaces with black people."[4]

74 WHAT ABOUT THE CHILDREN?

Finding spaces with Black or Hispanic or Asian people is essential for families with any BIPOC members. I don't just mean casually interacting with a few BIPOC adults in your church congregation or workplace, but intentionally placing your family in spaces with BIPOC peers, leaders, and influencers. The health of your adopted kids depends in part on them feeling good about the BIPOC part of themselves, and this requires being around positive BIPOC—on a regular basis.

Our country is still largely segregated, and it is still steeped in white supremacy. You can stand guard over what your kids watch on television when they're young, but in the age of the internet, the older they get, the more impossible this becomes. They will see negative depictions of people of color everywhere they turn, and if, on the other hand, everyone positive in their lives is white, they will think that white is better. They will gravitate toward all things white, and the more they do this, the more foreign BIPOC culture will become. Then if they happen to be in the company of Black people, for example, they will feel awkward, like imposters, and that will drive them toward the white world even more. It's a vicious cycle. This may work for a season, but the day will come when they realize they are not in fact white, and they will not know who they are, nor will they feel comfortable anywhere.

For adopted BIPOC, all of this is compounded by the fact that they were released for adoption by a person of color who couldn't raise them for whatever reason and then (90 percent of the time) adopted by a benevolent white family.[5] It would be easy to associate pain with one and kindness with the other. Dysfunction with one and virtue with the other. Add to that all the cultural racism we discussed in chapter 3, and you may end up with a child who is wrapped in Brown skin but who doesn't like Brown people.

I'm reminded of the powerful picture of the Black boy touching Barack Obama's hair in the Oval Office. *The most powerful man in the world has hair like mine!* I bet that little boy's life was forever altered. Who in your child's life has hair like theirs? Who do they see like them, not only in books, but up close and personal, who sees them, leads them, and influences them for good? In whose kitchen are they welcome, where the warmth and smells and flavors touch something deep within them, a neglected culture, perhaps, that they subliminally long for?

You cannot raise a child of color in an all-white world. It's just not fair.

People will move across the country for a job; will you move for your child? I know for some this is not possible. It may be impossible to move right now because of your job or an aging parent or some other reason, but diverse community is something your child needs for their psychological and emotional health, so think about it; pray about it. If you are a Christian, bring it to the Lord as you would any other of your children's needs and trust him to provide a solution. Just a short drive away from your present community there may be a more diverse club or sports team or a church with BIPOC leadership. Within these spaces you may find families to befriend; it may be awkward at first to reach out to them but please embrace awkwardness for the sake of your children. Your goal is to develop close friendships with families of color, not a pleasant hello in church, but intimate friends whom you and your children see often, where you feel at home in their home, and they feel at home in yours.

If you also have biological white children, it is also important for them to learn from people of color. If all they know is that their family "took in" a BIPOC kid, they may very well adopt a white savior mentality: *There's something wrong with Black and Brown people, so white people have to help them.* Your white children can develop a paternalistic attitude toward their nonwhite siblings: *Look what my family did for you!*

Your family is Mixed now, and your community needs to be Mixed too.

Adoption is a wonderful provision for children who are alone. God sets the solitary in families (Ps. 68:6). He set your BIPOC children in your family, and that is a beautiful thing. But these gorgeous children have needs that will require considerable change, including cultivating friendships with adults and kids who look like them. Nothing is impossible! God has already provided so much for your kids, and he will provide this too. Your job is to have your heart and eyes wide open, willing to do what it takes to raise grounded, happy kids.

Keep reading, as I discuss more about the importance of diverse community in the next two chapters.

QUESTIONS TO PONDER

1. What is your relationship like with your extended family —on both sides? Is it possible to see them more often?

2. How can you and your partner both be more involved in teaching your kids culture?

3. Have you and your partner been able to find a happy medium where your cultures collide?

4. How can you make time and allocate money to provide your kids with more cultural experiences?

STEPS FOR APPLICATION

Toddlers and Preschoolers

—Reflect. Do you know that your spouse or co-parent's culture is just as good and just as important as yours? If not, what interior work can you do to appreciate that culture more?

—In what ways are both of you imparting culture to your kids? How are you both rubbing off on your kids? If one of you usually cooks dinner, how are your kids learning the flavors of their other culture? What music do they hear? What kind of art do they see on your walls? Do they know the holidays, festivals, and traditions of both cultures?

—Tell your kids stories and legends from both cultures. If you or their grandparents migrated here, make sure your kids know how much courage that took. Let them know that those who came here or were brought here were heroes and sheroes because they survived.

Elementary School

—Determine if it is possible to visit extended family more. It's important for your kids to be in their BIPOC family's home: to smell the smells, hear the sounds, listen to the language and the accents, and take in the atmosphere.

—Each parent should take the kids to the library and choose books about their culture and then talk about those books with them. Similarly, take turns picking movies that teach things about your cultures.

YOU CAN'T DO IT ALONE! 79

—If one of you is from a non-English speaking country, what words and phrases can you teach your kids? Play music in the house with people singing in Spanish, or Chinese, or Hindi-Urdu—or wherever you are from—so that they can grow familiar with those sounds.

Tweens and Teens

—Each parent should constantly reinforce the beauty of all of your children's features. It would have been so significant if my dad had told me I was beautiful and if he had talked about the beauty of Black people in general.

—How can you make more room for your spouse or co-parent to impart life lessons to your teens? What do Black or Hispanic or Asian boys need to make it in this world? What practical things do you need to teach your Mixed-race girls?

VALUE III

Diversity

7

The Problem with Homogeneity

"I went to private schools full of white kids. I think a lot of that made me want to blend in or not be looked at as Black. The white kids are always talking about your hair and making you feel weird. I had this struggle of accepting myself as Black and loving that part of myself."

—Zoë Kravitz[1]

The third value we will discuss is *diversity*. Your family should not be the only source of diversity in your life. Do your children see you respecting and celebrating different cultures by actively participating in multiethnic communities?

Multiracial kids who grow up in a racially homogeneous world often want to blend in and look like the kids around them. They seek to assimilate, but assimilation is a lie that often leads to loneliness.

When I was old enough, I opted out of playing with the kids in the building and began venturing to a white friend's house to hang out after school and on the weekends. Laura lived in a gorgeous, multimillion-dollar brownstone, and I loved being there. We'd chat for hours, play with her (white) dolls, and watch TV. Her house was elegant and beautiful with every room perfectly appointed and kept immaculately clean by their maid. It was so different from my apartment, which was minimal and practical, our furniture purchased from Goodwill.

The more immersed I became in the white brownstone world, the more the Black kids in my building rejected me, and truth be told, I guess I rejected them too. The problem was, I envied Laura and wanted to be like her. I wished I had her sleek, long hair and her slender body; I felt ugly because I wasn't her and I wasn't white.

There is nothing new about adolescent angst over body type and physical appearance. I'm sure most teenage girls wish they looked like someone else. But there is additional anguish when you dislike yourself because you've subliminally absorbed ideas of racial inferiority. Parents of Mixed children, it's so important to be aware of this possibility and intentionally work to prevent it.

When I was with Laura and her friends, I felt less: less attractive, less acceptable, less worthy. Their world seemed better than mine. It was more beautiful, more wealthy, more lavish. Color and class were tangled up and interconnected in my mind, and my class and my color felt inferior to Laura's.

In her book *The Light We Carry*, Michelle Obama speaks of this. When she arrived at Princeton, she noted the confidence and entitlement of her white peers: "It hadn't dawned on me that the certainty and comfort being showcased by some of my peers were fed by an underground spring of generational wealth and deep networks of privilege."[2]

Laura's family enjoyed that underground spring, and mine did not.

Even though I felt different and inferior, my white friends seemed oblivious to my color—until we hit adolescence and white boys entered the scene. These boys were not oblivious, and they let me know there was no way they would date a Black girl. When I was younger, Black kids rejected me because I wasn't Black enough. Now in adolescence, white boys rejected me because I wasn't white enough.

In the decade of the seventies, that iconic poster of Farrah Fawcett with her long blond hair and that red bathing suit was the standard of beauty. I don't remember a single Black woman in mainstream media who was considered beautiful. They certainly existed: Diana Ross, Jayne Kennedy, Beverly Johnson (who in 1974 became the first Black woman on the cover of *Vogue* magazine), but in the white world I usually

THE PROBLEM WITH HOMOGENEITY 85

inhabited, white women were considered the most beautiful, and I could aspire to look nothing like them.

Again, in *The Light We Carry*, Michelle Obama writes, "When you look around and can't find any version of yourself out there in the wider world, when you scan the horizon and see nobody like you, you start to feel a broader loneliness, a sense of being mismatched to your hopes, your own plans, your own strengths. You begin to wonder where—and how—you will ever belong."[3]

Similarly, Tasha Jun writes, "I've always felt unfit as a Korean but somehow too Korean everywhere else."[4] I can relate to that so much! I felt unfit as a Black person, but too Black to truly fit in with white people.

My friend Melody, who is biracial Korean like Jun, told me that when her mom came to America from Korea and married her white dad, she wanted her kids to assimilate into white culture. They lived in white communities, first in Mississippi and then in western New York. Her mom experienced so much racism because of her thick accent that she didn't want her daughters to experience that pain too. The message Melody received was, "I want you to be American (white). I do not want you to be Korean. I want you to have American names. I don't want you to speak like a Korean. You need to be American." There was a sense that to be successful in America, you had to be as white as possible. Melody knows that her mom was just trying to protect her kids; she had her own trauma from growing up in war-torn Korea, and she was so relieved to be in America. She just wanted her kids to have an easier life, but Melody, who looks more Asian than white, still experienced racism, and since she had not been taught to be proud of her Korean heritage, she wound up wishing she wasn't Korean. For her, Korean meant rejection, and so she tried to distance herself from her Korean heritage. "I got the message: Korean's bad, Asian's bad. . . . So I would stare at myself in the mirror and just try to open my eyes really wide thinking that I could look whiter."

Malcolm X said in a 1962 rally,

Who taught you, please, who taught you to hate the texture of your hair? Who taught you to hate the color of your skin to such extent that you bleach to get like the white man? Who taught you to hate the shape of your nose and the shape of your lips? Who taught you to hate yourself from the top of your head to the soles of your feet? Who taught you to hate your own kind?[5]

America taught us that.

Melody finally began to feel comfortable in her skin when she attended a diverse college and found peers who looked like her. She delighted to be around so many kinds of people with different colors, religions, cultures, and stories. In college, she finally began to like herself.

Melody's story is not usual. When many immigrants arrive here, the message they receive directly or indirectly from other immigrants is, "Keep your head down, work hard, and assimilate." They believe that through assimilation they will belong and succeed.

I remember talking with a Ghanaian friend many years ago. She admitted that when she was getting ready to come to the States, her parents told her to make only white friends. They told her that Black Americans were lazy and that making white friends would lead to success. Many people in majority-Black and -Brown countries underestimate the severity of racism in the United States because they have never experienced it; they believe that America is a wealthy land of opportunity where all have equal access to that opportunity, so poverty must be a by-product of laziness. They see the stereotyped depictions of Black people in movies and television shows that get exported all over the world and believe that Black Americans are indolent criminals. When you're from a nonwhite country, it's easy to dismiss the advantage of being in the majority, of never having to prove your worth despite your race, of never having your soul sullied by white supremacy. These immigrants arrive and try to build primarily white friendships, but then they slowly begin to feel loneliness as they realize they aren't fully understood or accepted by their white friends, and yet they have distanced themselves from other people of color.

We all try to assimilate to some degree when we're visiting a different country or when we're amid a different culture. For example, years ago, I spent a summer in China and quickly learned to take off my shoes and leave them outside the door when I entered someone's home. I did this out of respect: *When in Rome*, as they say. This is proper and right. But the kind of assimilation that leads you to completely reject your own culture and try to replace it with another that you consider superior to your own—all because you so desperately want to fit in—is toxic.

This brings up the negative side of code-switching. (We looked at the more positive motivations in chapter 5.) Code-switching is damaging if we feel as if who we are is undesirable and inferior to the dominant culture. "This [is the] kind of code-switching that leaves people feeling as if they're not acceptable the way that they are. The damage comes less from the shift in behavior and more from the pressure to maintain an inauthentic facade."[6] Or, as Dr. Beverly Tatum writes, "Trying to find common ground with others is not harmful by itself. . . . It becomes harmful if you have to deny your own sense of identity in order to do so."[7]

Parents, when your children are around a certain racial group, do they seem to hide themselves and attempt to become someone else? Do they seem to fear that drawing attention to their ethnicity will put them at a disadvantage—socially, academically, professionally? Most kids act goofy around their friends, but do you notice such a dramatic shift in your kids that you barely recognize them? In this case, code-switching ceases to be normal and becomes a desperate and toxic attempt to assimilate.

When you code-switch and try to assimilate into white culture, for example, you closet your BIPOC ethnicity, you gravitate toward white people, white music, art, fashion, beauty standards. You read books written only by white people, you believe that white is better, and although your skin may not be white, you try to become white in every other way. You deny your nonwhite heritage, wishing it weren't there, willing it gone, and you lose yourself.

Jun writes, "I've believed the lie of assimilation and white supremacy until it led me to a dead end. I couldn't grow or be known by assimilating. I couldn't experience being loved when part of me was pushed aside. The isolation I experienced from putting to death the details God intentionally placed in me eventually broke me."[8]

Well said. It broke me too.

The current's pull toward white preference is strong, and the lie that lighter is better permeates our ideas of beauty, morality, and character and manifests in every corner of our culture. This, coupled by the relative wealth of white communities compared to communities of color, can make it easy for kids who are partly white to prefer all things white and tacitly wish to be white. Especially if they live in white neighborhoods, attend white schools, and have mostly white friends, they can begin to reject the BIPOC part of themselves and simply want to become as white as possible. Added to this, if they have white extended family members who are more affluent than nonwhite extended family members, this, too, can make kids believe white is better.

In parenting my sons, I've thought a lot about the issue of believing that white is better and wishing to assimilate. We live in a very white suburb and a very white school district, and I've been concerned that my kids would try to somehow closet their blackness, especially as they began to experience racism.

One son went to his first birthday party when he was three. We knew he'd be the only Black kid because the party guests were all from his preschool class, which was all white—except him. Ten minutes into the party, the host gathered the wiggly three-year-olds into a circle and explained the rules of *Duck, Duck, Goose*. The birthday girl went first, and as she worked her way around the circle, tapping heads, I noticed that each time she arrived at my son's head, she passed her hand over it,

THE PROBLEM WITH HOMOGENEITY

never touching it. She tapped the next kid's head and the next and finally jubilantly shouted *GOOSE*! She took off around the circle, gleefully chased by the new kid up, and then breathlessly slid into the open spot, triumphant for having made it around. When this next child got to my son's head, he too passed over it, refusing to touch it. Kid after kid did the same thing. Nine out of ten kids got to be *Goose* that day—every child except my son.

I've seen so many memes to the effect, "Kids aren't born racist; they are taught to be so." I disagree. I am sure no parent sat their squirmy three-year-old down and said, "Now, Johnny, don't touch that little Black boy's head!" Rather, these kids saw that my son was *different*, and they all subconsciously, on their own, decided to avoid touching *different*. He was invited to the party but was never fully included.

A friend has a similar story of her Black son hitting homerun after homerun on his mostly white baseball team, cheered on at the games, but never invited to the team parties. BIPOC kids in all white spaces often struggle to make close friendships, and this intensifies as they approach adolescence. Black and white kids have played together for centuries, even on plantations where the Black kids were enslaved, but the division comes with adolescence. When they begin to become young adults, sometimes they simply drift apart. Latent racism within themselves or their parents begins to surface and makes the relationship too difficult.

My kids have been called *monkey*, *dirty*, and *muddy* countless times. They've been told that their skin resembled *poop* and that they looked like gang members. At mostly white summer camps, kids have queried if they were from the inner city or perhaps from another country all together. It has been so evident that these white kids live highly segregated lives and have never been in the company of Black people.

Because of where we live, we've been very intentional about teaching the beauty of Black culture. We watch Black movies, read Black books, listen to Black music, and hang Black art on our walls. When we looked around and realized that despite all of these things, almost every person of influence in our kids lives was white, we changed our church membership to a Black church with Black leadership so that every Sunday and sometimes during the week they are saturated in Black culture and witness Black excellence. They see Black achievement not just in books but also all around them on Sunday mornings.

Parents of Mixed-race kids, it is your job to build community with diverse people. I shared that I grew up in Brooklyn, which is the opposite of the Rochester suburbs as it is one of the most diverse cities in the world. But even in diverse cities, segregation thrives. Economics, school districting, and cultural preferences separate people. You can live in the middle of Chicago or New York and still stick with your coworkers who look like you and socialize after hours only with those of the same background. You can live on an island of homogeneity amid a sea of diversity.

Because I felt rejected by my Black peers, I hung out with white kids, and for reasons I may never know, my parents befriended only white people. We attended majority-white churches with white leadership. We went to a white family's house every year for Thanksgiving. We never had a Black family over nor did we observe the inside of Black family life. My parents became good friends with the white women who lived next door and these women became aunties to us, but we had no Black aunties. Even in a place like Brooklyn, diverse community takes intentionality, and though my parents were intentional about some things, they were not intentional about this.

Whether you live in a big city or a small town, humility and intentionality are crucial: humility to know you *need* close friendships with diverse people and intentionality because the effort will likely require discomfort.

So, what do you do? You put yourself in spaces where making diverse friends is possible. If your kids see *you* appreciating multiple cultures, they will appreciate them too. Despite fear or nervousness, invite these friends over and then go to their house if they invite you. Make sure your kids are not only exposed to but also often surrounded by good role models who are Black, Asian, or Hispanic. Read the books, watch the movies, nurture the friendships. If your kids are never shown the beauty

THE PROBLEM WITH HOMOGENEITY 91

of their BIPOC heritage and if they see only racism and cultural stereotypes, they might end up being drawn to a defiant, antiwhite subculture or rejecting their BIPOC heritage all together.

Knowing Who You Are

I want to end this chapter recounting two ancient stories you may be familiar with. I'm sharing them because they speak to assimilation. The first is Moses' story. During the four hundred years of the Israelites' enslavement in Egypt, the Israelites grew in number, to the point that the Egyptians felt threatened. In response, Pharoah ordered the murder of all male Hebrew babies. He told the midwives to kill them as they emerged from the womb. The midwives refused to do this, and Moses was born, despite the most powerful empire on the planet trying to prevent it. (Among other things, this shows us the power of resistance even from the obscure.) But when his mother could no longer hide him, she put him in a basket and set him adrift in the reeds along the Nile.

As providence would have it, Pharoah's daughter found him and adopted him (even hiring Moses' mother to nurse him). Moses was raised by Egyptians; he learned their language and their customs. He had access to power and privilege. He dressed like them, spoke like them, and I'm sure in many ways thought like them, but he had not entirely become Egyptian.

One day, when he saw an Egyptian mistreating an enslaved Israelite, indignation rose in his belly; he became so enraged that he killed the Egyptian. Moses could have turned away and headed back to the palace. He may have felt badly, but he could have chosen to do nothing, but he never forgot who he was. The Hebrews were his people, and when he saw one of his countrymen being beaten, deep called unto deep, and he had to act. He looked Egyptian, but he was not Egyptian; he was a Jew from the tribe of Levi.

Similarly, when the Jews were exiled in Persia, Hadassah was taken from her Uncle Mordecai's home to be part of King

Xerxes's harem. She, too, dwelt in a palace, with access to the most exquisite jewelry, fragrant perfumes, beautiful clothes, and sumptuous food, and she took a new name, Esther, so that no one knew her true Jewish identity. (Mind you, no one should envy Esther's position because she was essentially a sex-slave; nevertheless, God used her at that time and in that place.)

One day, Mordecai found out about a plot to kill all the Jews in the empire, and he implored Esther to help. He asked her to beseech the king on behalf of her people. Like Moses, Esther could have turned away. No one knew she was Jewish, so even if all the Jews were killed, she probably would have survived. But once again, deep called unto deep, and she remembered who she was. She was not Esther; she was Hadassah, niece of Mordecai, from the tribe of Benjamin. Her people were in trouble, and she risked her life to help them.

Both Moses and Esther enjoyed privileged lives, proximity to power, removal from suffering, but even with all of that, they didn't forget who they were. They could have identified with the powerful, but they chose to identify with the powerless. Jesus did this too: "Though he was God, he did not think of equality with God as something to cling to. Instead, he gave up his divine privileges; he took the humble position of a slave and was born as a human being" (Phil 2:6–7 NLT).

Some may accuse your Mixed-race child of being a sellout because they have the privilege that comes with lighter skin, but this doesn't make her a sellout. Not being able to speak Spanish, or having straighter hair, or preferring classical music: these don't make your child a sellout. Tell your kids this is rubbish! Rather, a sellout is someone who has striven so hard to assimilate with the majority culture that he has forgotten that the man in the chokehold, or the young woman languishing at the border, or the old woman wiping from her face spit hurled from lips curled in xenophobic hatred could be their father, their brother, their aunt, their grandmother. A sellout is someone who looks away and pretends that this couldn't possibly be them.

QUESTIONS TO PONDER

1. Do you see your kids changing themselves to try to fit in with other kids? What behaviors or lingo do they adopt? What part of themselves are they trying to highlight or hide?

2. Are your kids embarrassed about their home or extended family, the smells, accents, art, or food that make their family different from their peers? What can you do to help them feel proud about this part of themselves?

3. What BIPOC people of influence or leadership do your children have in their lives?

4. What is your kids' response to racist incidents in the news?

STEPS FOR APPLICATION

Toddlers and Preschoolers

—Talk to your little ones about the care God took in making the world so multifaceted and diverse. Help them to see how boring it would be if there were only one kind of flower, one kind of tree, one kind of food, one kind of fish. God also made people diverse with all different eye shapes, eye color, skin color, and hair texture, and it is all *very* good.

—Play silly games with your kids, like asking them how crazy it would be if a mouse tried to be an elephant or if a dog tried to meow like a cat. That's how silly it would be if they tried to look or act like someone else. God made them unique; there is only one person in all the world like them!

Elementary School

—Do a family tree with your children and tell stories along the way. Tell them about a grandparent who arrived speaking no English or an uncle who marched during the civil rights movement. Boast about these family members and help your children realize how brave, persevering, and resilient they were. Tell them about a white grandfather who fought in WWII or helped organize a labor union. In this way, they can take pride in both sides of their family. Let your kids know that without these relatives' sacrifices, they wouldn't enjoy some of the privileges that they have. *All* these stories make your kids who they are, and they are part of long, rich family lines. If they have family members with less positive stories because of bad choices, deemphasize those for now, and later, when your kids are older, gradually tell them about those

THE PROBLEM WITH HOMOGENEITY 95

more difficult stories. Demonstrate compassion and help them to understand some of the reasons for their dysfunction. Help your kids recognize that we are all flawed and that we all make bad decisions sometimes.

— Think about the racial and ethnic demographic of your church, neighborhood, children's school, and the people your kids mostly stick with. Do you notice them trying to be like other kids? Some of this is natural but not if it means rejecting their cultural heritage. If you notice this, actively, intentionally help to facilitate friendships between your kids and kids with some of their same heritage.

— Help your kids to know what a true friend is: a true friend is someone who likes and appreciates them for who they are. Reassure them that they don't need lots of friends. Rather, a few true friends is plenty.

— Help your kids to take pride in the things that make them different from their friends. If they bring a different type of lunch to school (kimchee, curry, rice and beans), encourage them that it may be different from their friends' food, but it is delicious! Similarly, if their grandmother wears a saree or speaks with a thick accent, for example, tell them often how beautiful these clothes are and how smart grandma is for knowing two (or more!) languages. If your kids seem reluctant to invite their friends to your house, ask them why. Let them know that their *halmeoni*, their *abuela*, their *nani*, the smell of curry in their home, the pictures on their walls, all these things make your family beautiful and special.

Tweens and Teens

— Check on your tweens and teens regularly to see if they are finding community with kids who look like them, and if they are not, do what it takes to help them find it. Do you have to drive them across town to a different sports league? Do you have to change churches? Do you have to move? Should you invest in a summer camp where they might enjoy friendship with kids who look like them? Helping your kids find their crew will be worth any sacrifice you make. Do what it takes to keep your kids from sliding into isolation and loneliness.

8

The Beauty of Diversity

> I went to Howard, and that really changed the way that I
> was able to identify with the Black part of me. . . . There
> were so many mixes, and with so many different countries, so
> many different socioeconomic backgrounds. I really felt really
> accepted and loved for the first time.
>
> —Thema, Black and Chicana[1]

Michelle Obama writes this about college: "It dumps a lot of new people in front of you, rearranging your notions of what's possible, often blowing the lid off whatever you thought didn't or couldn't exist."[2]

Dartmouth did that for me. I still use the Bible that a Black college friend gave me one year for my birthday, she spoke fluent Chinese and wrote an inscription in Chinese characters on the front page. A Chinese-speaking Black woman, she was fully grounded in her Black identity, but being Black was multifaceted for her. There was no one way; it was not monolithic. *Black* was not a single story.

In her TedTalk, novelist Chimamanda Ngozi Adichie speaks of the danger of "the single story." She talks about growing up in a middle-class family in Nigeria. Like most middle-class families, hers had a houseboy who lived with them. His name was Fide, and the only thing Adichie's mother told her about Fide was that he was very poor, so she felt only enormous pity for him. And then one day they visited Fide in his home, and his mother showed them a beautiful basket Fide's brother had made. Adichie admits that she was surprised because it had never occurred to her that anyone in Fide's family could create something beautiful. "All I heard about them was how poor they were, so that it became impossible for me to see them as anything else but poor. Their poverty was my single story of them."[3]

When Adichie came to the States, she had to deal with America's single story of Africa: that Africans fight senseless wars and die of poverty and AIDS. Americans rarely learn any other story of Africa, and yet there are so many other stories, both tragic and beautiful. She reminds us that it is the powerful who control what stories we hear: what books are chosen for school curricula, what movies are produced, what books are published, what articles see the light of day. In America, most of those with the power to choose are white, some of whom want only the stories of Black and Brown dysfunction told. Some want only our victimization told, and some want only our guilt told, but either way, these single stories dehumanize us and rob us of our dignity.

When we don't know any Black people, our single story of them might be that they are poor underachievers, or unintelligent, or dangerous. When we don't know any Hispanic people, our single story of them might be that they are undocumented refugees, trying to fleece our medical system. When we don't know any Asians, our single story of them might be that they are quiet, submissive, or good at math.

My experience growing up taught me that there was only one way to be Black, and since I wasn't that way, I couldn't be Black. But college introduced me to Black people who did not fit that mold either and yet were very proudly Black. My single story of blackness disintegrated.

My Black friends didn't care that I listened to classical music; many of them did, too, and they also loved to turn the bass up and jam to a new gospel beat. They didn't care that I had white friends; they had white friends too. They didn't care that I couldn't dance; they knew that being Black was so much bigger than that. In college, I came to experience and love a multifaceted blackness, and my skin became a source of pride, rather than an albatross of shame.

THE BEAUTY OF DIVERSITY

While living in that community, I joined a gospel choir, and I remember the day I looked around, astounded by the beauty of the Black women who sang with me. Their bodies were womanly, curvy, beautiful. They didn't aspire to shapelessness like so many of my white friends seemed to, but they clothed themselves with courageous, colorful dignity and with garments that hugged rather than hid every curve. There was nothing about them that shrank back; they stepped forward into the sun, knowing their worth and splendor. Their lips bold, painted red and purple and brown—distinct, not demure. They seemed so comfortable in their skin, so self-assured, so grounded.

I had been surrounded by whiteness my entire life, and I had adopted the white standard of beauty. These women challenged it, defied it. I didn't even sing very well, but within that group, I began to love me.

In college, I read African American literature, which drew me in like an embrace. I loved the way these authors used words: assonance, aphorism, alliteration. Frederick Douglass, George Moses Horton, Paul Laurence Dunbar, David Walker, William Wells Brown, Francis Ellen Watkins Harper, Sojourner Truth, Malcolm X. Where had these writers been all my life? It was as if I had dwelt in a world of only a few colors, and then someone opened the door and I glimpsed through it reds and blues and yellows and oranges for the first time. The universe was so much bigger, so much more wonderfully complex than I had imagined.

During that season, I began to identify as a Black woman. I wasn't ashamed of my mom, but I had come to realize that the world saw me as Black, and I liked that. I admired Black people and viewed them as one of the most resilient peoples on the planet. I learned about Black architects who helped to design some of our national treasures, Black mathematicians who enabled men to orbit the moon, Black inventors who rescued economies, Black writers who penned brilliant prose, Black preachers whose oratory skills remain unrivaled.

Black people were there, performing breakthrough surgeries, inventing blood banks, and exploring barren wildernesses. We

100 WHAT ABOUT THE CHILDREN?

were there, winning Nobel Peace Prizes, Pulitzer Prizes, Oscars, Tonys, Emmys, Grammys, breaking barriers, pressed down and rising still. Every "you can't" became "watch me," and every negative assumption was disproven and rejected for the lie that it was.

You can't swim. You can't play tennis. You can't play golf. You can't quarterback. You can't play classical music or dance ballet. You can't pilot a plane or a fighter jet. You can't lead a company. You can't lead a country. You can't lead a family. You can't excel in math or science. You can't direct a movie or produce a film. You can't write a bestseller. You can't make wealth. You can't argue a case. You can't think logically or rationally. You can't demonstrate courage.

Oh yes, we can. We did all those things—and we are still doing them. I no longer wanted to closet or diminish the Black in me. I owned it, relished in it, and felt intense pride about it.

It took leaving my family home and going to college to love blackness, but your kids can discover this kind of pride much sooner; their story doesn't have to be one of painful self-rejection until one day, hopefully, they learn to like themselves.

Immersing them in all parts of their culture sets them up to learn self-acceptance earlier. Surrounding them with diverse family and friends will help them to embrace all of themselves from a young age. And by diversity, I mean not just racial and ethnic diversity, but also economic diversity and diversity of thought. Some of my Black friends came from wealthy families and some from poor families. Some would be first-generation college graduates and some second-generation. Some were athletes and some nerds, some studied humanities, and others science.

It was in college that Psalm 139:14 began to travel deeper into my soul. "Thank you for making me so wonderfully complex! Your workmanship is marvelous—how well I know it" (NLT). It didn't happen overnight, but I did finally begin to know that I was wonderfully complex.

When we see all different kinds of people, we are more likely to find people who are like us and who appreciate us for who we are. When we're around only one kind of person and we don't fit in, we feel lost and alone. Your children will count the number of kids who look like them in a room, and if they can count no one, they will instantly, though probably subliminally, feel different, like they stand out in all the wrong ways, and they will feel isolated. Their attempts to fit in will be all the more poignant, and when they don't fully fit in, their dejection will be that much deeper.

Your children aren't fully white or fully Black or fully Asian or fully Hispanic; they are complex, and they will need a broad, generous community to find belonging. Leaving home often enables this, but it can happen earlier.

I spoke with a white friend who made an important decision about community. She has a Black husband and four biracial children, and they live in a mostly white suburb outside of Chicago. For a while, they cast around looking for a good church and finally settled on a large, Black church in Chicago, forty minutes away. She knew it was important for her husband to find a place where he could exhale, especially after the racial turmoil of 2020. They both wanted a pastor who understood and ministered to the pain of racism. And they also wanted their children to sit under Black authority and more regularly experience Black excellence and Black culture. At first, my friend was aware of how much she stood out, and she wondered why the church, though affluent and progressive, didn't provide hymnals or project the words of songs on screens; instead, the church remained committed to the call-and-response worship style of old. Now she is accustomed to it and considers the benefits to herself and her family far greater than any initial discomfort.

I have another white friend who, when she and her husband adopted two biracial boys, sold their home in an all-white school district and moved to a more diverse one. In their new school, their boys have some BIPOC teachers and BIPOC friends, and they feel more comfortable because they stand out less.

My racial identity journey continued after college, even though I still lived in New Hampshire, a very white state. College and military towns often attract diversity because both actively recruit people of color. (They also often have a hard time *retaining* BIPOC, but that topic is for another day.) Hanover, New Hampshire, is no exception. After graduating, I started working in full-time ministry, leading outreach projects, pastoring a student church, teaching, and wearing about a hundred hats, which is typical for nonprofit organizations. I had both close white friends and close friends of color as diverse people came to Dartmouth for postgraduate studies or to join the faculty or to work in the area for other reasons. Meeting so many kinds of people began to open my mind to new thoughts.

I grew up in a politically liberal home and then went to a liberal college and attended a conservative church. Members were outspoken about pro-life and other conservative issues, and I jumped in and became vocal about these things too. But as I read more and talked more to my BIPOC friends, my political worldview changed yet again.

My white friends were largely conservative Christians, and though most of my Black friends were also Christians, they voted very differently. There was an assumption of assimilation among some of my white friends: if you are a true Christian, you will be a conservative. All was well when I adopted those views, but as I began to question things, this created stress within some of those relationships.

I remember a conversation I had with a white friend who spoke about the 1960s in a very disparaging way. In his opinion, that decade was all about rebellion. I don't think it ever occurred to him that without the gains of the '60s, I may not even have been there. He and so many others did not grasp the profundity of that time: the bombings, firehoses, marches, and billy clubs, the courage of John Lewis on that bridge, the miracle of nonviolent protest amid vigilante executions, and the slaughter of four little girls in a Baptist church.

I remember explaining why Malcolm took "X" as his last name and what racists had done to his mom and dad. The more I thought, read, and spoke with Black friends, the more I began to chafe. As a Christian, why did I have to revere Ronald

THE BEAUTY OF DIVERSITY

Reagan? Did God care only about the baby in the womb? Didn't he also care about Rodney King, who received such a savage beating from those who swore to serve and protect? Was his life not equally important? Didn't that event deserve outrage too? Why were conservatives so quiet about racism? Didn't they understand that for so many people, the "good ol' days" were not so good?

Having said all of that, I also later realized that racism is no respecter of political party. Over the years, I've met just as many liberals as conservatives who have never had a Black neighbor or a Black friend and who would be distressed if their school district rezoned to include more Black and Brown kids or if affordable housing replaced some of the green space in their neighborhood. Moreover, progressives can be so focused on Black persecution that they pigeonhole Black people as perpetual underachievers and are completely unaware of Black excellence. It's as if they don't want to even see it because it disrupts their narrative of Black oppression. They remove all human agency and reduce Black people to one-dimensional victims. This robs Black people of human dignity as much as believing that all Black people are criminals.

It's also important to realize that both parties seek Black and Brown loyalty and desire Black and Brown people to fit neatly into the categories they have created. Yet, truth be told, many people of color feel politically homeless because we subscribe wholeheartedly to neither party. Honestly, I don't think any of us should subscribe wholeheartedly to either party. Humanity is flawed, and vice and virtue dwell equally on both sides of the aisle. That doesn't mean we all have to be political independents, but it does mean we should see some good in what each party has to offer.

A few months ago, we had a Black family over for dinner, and the wife expressed that she is a Republican. She believes very much in racial justice and speaks passionately against systemic racism, but on other issues, she is more conservative. My sons' eyes grew wide: *"You're a Republican?"* They didn't think Black people could be Republicans! Later when we talked about it, one son admitted that it was refreshing to know this because he, too, has some conservative ideas. I was happy that he was affirmed in this way. Just by having this couple over, he realized in a deeper way that it was OK to be who he is.

Why am I talking about politics? Because your children's racial identity journey will undoubtedly include a political identity journey—race and politics are intertwined. Historically, political parties fought to keep and end slavery, maintain and demolish segregation, curb and increase racial profiling, end and preserve affirmative action, increase and decrease immigration, encourage and discourage languages other than English, and champion scores of other things that directly affect Black and Brown people. As your children grapple with who they are racially and ethnically, they will probably also grapple with what they believe politically, especially as teenagers and young adults. Don't be afraid of this, but rather listen and help them to think critically. Perhaps they will end up embracing some of both, which I think is a good thing. Your kids will be a lot of *boths,* and they may be politically both too.

Parents, are you willing to be uncomfortable so that your children can be comfortable? Are you willing to expand your world and intentionally make close friendships so that your kids regularly see people who look like them in your home? Are you willing to change churches or even move for the sake of your kids? Can you listen to different ideas, different opinions, without jumping to the conclusion that this person must not be a true Christian, or a true American, or a true person of color?

To be grounded, stable and secure, kids need a lot of scaffolding: different kinds of folks who look like them surrounding them, loving them, encouraging them, and honoring them. Before they launch out into the world, they have to know that they are beautiful, smart human beings. People may clutch their bags or do a quick, nervous double take when they pass. A teacher or a professor may assume that they will underachieve. Adults may botch their names, and kids may laugh at their food. They need to hear from you and from others that they are not less. As a matter of fact, they are great.

QUESTIONS TO PONDER

1. How often do you get together with friends who have a different worldview from you? Are you able to talk about your differences and learn from each other?

2. If you are religious, what religious values do you see in our political parties? How do your faith and values influence your politics?

3. In what ways have you embraced discomfort so that your kids can be comfortable?

4. What kind of scaffolding do your children have?

STEPS FOR APPLICATION

Toddlers and Preschoolers

— Before approaching your kids, do a little self-examination first. What single stories of folks do you have? (We all have them.) Do you think Black equals poor, Hispanic equals drugs, Asian equals stern? Be aware that even the Asian "model minority" stereotype is harmful because it reduces an entire people group, consisting of over four billion people, to one thing. God created multidimensional people, and to think of anyone as one-dimensional robs that person of her worth. Once you're grounded in that truth, it will be easier to teach your kids that truth.

— Find picture books that tell a different story. For example, disrupt the single story of Black people being good at only sports and music or Hispanics being poor and undocumented by reading picture books about Black and Hispanic inventors, scientists, and leaders.

Elementary School

— During school breaks, provide books for your kids that disrupt single stories. For example, if they know only about Black athletes, give them books about Black inventors. If they are unaware of Hispanic thinkers, give them books about them and then ask questions. Similarly, as a family, watch movies about famous BIPOC and discuss them afterward.

— Think about economic and political diversity. How often do your kids get to hear economically or politically diverse people talk and share their views in constructive ways? Whom can you befriend and invite over who is different from you in this way?

THE BEAUTY OF DIVERSITY 107

—Be careful not to disparage those who are different from you politically or economically. Little ears will pick up negative bias, and this can predispose them to being judgmental.

Tweens and Teens

—Invite someone over for dinner whose story is different from the single story your children may believe. Coach your kids beforehand to listen and ask good questions.

—Talk to your kids about politics. Let them know that there is good in both parties and that both parties reflect some good values. Also, neither party is fully righteous because no one is fully righteous. Your household is ethnically and racially complex, and it is very possible that it will also be politically complex, and that is a good thing!

—Watch movies and documentaries about leaders whose politics may be different from your own. You and your kids can learn together about people who had a different worldview from you but who did important things. Your goal is to help your kids think critically and to resist the tribalism so rife in our culture.

VALUE IV

Honesty

9

Be Honest with Yourself

> For all intents and purposes, my brother and I were raised with no connection to being Japanese. . . . [My father's] experience growing up in rural Minnesota being called every racial slur under the sun, I think there's trauma there. I think my parents operated to try and raise us to have a better and easier life
> —Josh, Caucasian and Japanese[1]

The fourth value we're going to talk about is *honesty*: being honest with yourself and honest with your kids. The older your kids get, the more they need to know how they may be perceived in the wider world and how to handle it when those perceptions are negative. But before you're honest with them, you have to be honest with yourself. Do you harbor any racial bigotry or racial trauma? Just because you have Mixed-race kids does not mean you are free from racism. You can marry a person of another race and subconsciously think that he is the exception to the rule. And you can certainly sleep with someone and believe this. Racism has never hindered sexual desire.

Added to that, many BIPOC harbor racial trauma from their past, and if they don't deal with it, it will negatively affect their parenting. It certainly affected my father's ability to parent us well.

In 1975, I didn't like coming home from school. Like a lot of kids, I looked forward to settling down to the *Brady Bunch—Gilligan's Island—I Love Lucy* trio before tackling my homework. I knew practically every line of every episode and could sing their ballad jingles in my sleep. But I didn't like it

112 WHAT ABOUT THE CHILDREN?

that my dad was nearly always home (that is, not at a job) and nearly always on the phone.

Hello, this is Ted Lewis. May I speak to your manager?

Two things bothered me about this one-sided conversation. First, my dad was attempting self-employment again, trying to sell his latest idea; and second, his name wasn't Ted Lewis. When making his pitch on the phone, he morphed from the dark, Harlem-born Austin Leonard to the preppy, white Ted Lewis in hopes of getting more sales.

My father was raised with the mantra "If you want to succeed in life, you have to be as white as possible." In person, with his six-foot-two, three-hundred-pound frame, he could con no one; but on the phone he could be white, and he made more sales. I hated this act. Most kids want their fathers to be powerful, and this charade made him seem servile. These attempts at self-employment always ended in failure, which soaked into his soul, leaving him depressed and my mother resentful.

Some of my dad's employment issues stemmed from his time at Fort Carson. He grew up in Harlem in the 1940s and '50s, surrounded by Black people, and his parents tried to shelter him from the realities of racism. They led him to believe that if he talked right and lived right, he would be accepted into the white world, and everything would be just fine. That, of course, was not true, and when he left Harlem, he was set adrift in a world he didn't understand.

He was drafted during the Vietnam years, when a disproportionate number of draftees were Black, a disproportionate number of those sent to the front lines were Black, and a disproportionate number of those denied support by Veterans Affairs were Black. Thankfully, my dad was honorably discharged only days before his regiment was sent overseas. While enlisted, though, he experienced the most rabid of racism. As far as his commanding officer was concerned, his name was only Monkey N-word. His CO targeted him, dehumanized him, and broke him. His perfect diction and manners didn't shield him from toxic hatred, and I have often wondered if he suffered from PTSD from that experience.

My dad was never taught to take pride in being Black, and when he was targeted because he was Black, he had no idea how to deal with it. Racism crushed his soul, and he shut that pain away in a dark closet and locked the door. But pain shut in closets doesn't stay there. It finds ways to seep through the cracks and taint everything in its path. My dad spent his entire adulthood trying to dodge demons of inferiority and prove that he was somebody, but the legal racism, systemic racism, and cultural racism of the 1940s, '50s, and '60s conspired together and compromised his physical, emotional, and mental health. I really believe he thought the only way to make something of his life was to be on his own, making his way as his own boss, out from under the white man's gaze—but he just couldn't figure out how to do that.

For centuries, Black men were treated as inferior and unintelligent, and when their failures seemed to confirm this, it devastated them. Personal shame combined with generational shame and stymied resilience for some, rendering success more difficult than it should have been.

My mother grew up very differently. In her world, men worked, and women stayed at home. In Black families, few Black men were granted the opportunity to make enough money so that their wives could stay at home. But in the white world, in the era in which my mom came of age, even blue-collar white men earned enough to support their families. My mom expected to be a housewife, and my dad couldn't figure out how to make money.

It would have been great for my dad to seek healing from his past: he had grown up in poverty, then was targeted and shut out of satisfying jobs because of his color. But there really wasn't a place for Black men to go to seek healing back then. Therapy was only for rich white people, his parents shut away their own pain and didn't discuss it, and the white pastors of the churches my parents attended wouldn't have known how to help him even if he had dug deep and bared his soul. My father was a perfect example of generational trauma resulting in dysfunction, and that left him incapable of helping me with my own racial identity.

Sometimes immigrants from poor or war-torn countries also carry trauma from growing up with the constant threat of danger. When they come to the United States, they try to leave all that grief behind, and they present a front of joy and optimism to their kids. But this kind of denial of their past and naivety that all will be well now that they are in America can handicap their parenting and make them less effective than if they were candid about their experiences and taught their kids from a place of honesty and truth.

When I see interracial couples, my heart smiles. Here is a couple whose love triumphed over the racial bias so deeply rooted in our culture. As Maya Angelou wrote, "Love recognizes no barriers. It jumps hurdles, leaps fences, penetrates walls to arrive at its destination full of hope."[2] Some are daunted by racial hurdles, but others face them bravely, and that is a beautiful thing. Marriage can be difficult for anyone, but when you add cultural difference and racial trauma, there's even more to understand and work through. But this can make interracial marriages some of the strongest. You've embarked on an adventure to understand, respect, and embrace all the subtle and not-so-subtle cultural nuances and experiences of the person you vowed to love and cherish. How rich to plumb the depths of each other's upbringing and worldview and pass on the best of what you find to your kids.

But sometimes interracial couples struggle specifically because of unhealed racial wounds. Some BIPOC men have internalized white supremacy, that is, white is better and therefore white women are better, so they marry white women partly out of self-rejection. They don't like being Black or Brown, and they hope that white wives will help them to merge into whiteness. They believe these women will elevate their social status and garner them respect. The difficulty is if the white women they marry don't understand or empathize with what they've been through, their search for respect can end in frustration and bitterness.

Ta-Nehisi Coates writes this about Barack Obama:

He married a black woman. It is easy to forget how shocking this was, given the common belief at the time that there was a direct relationship between success and assimilation. The narrative held that successful black men took white wives and crossed over into that arid no-man's-land that was not black, though it could never be white. Blackness for such men was not a thing to root yourself in but something to evade and escape.[3]

I have sometimes wondered if my dad was trying to evade and escape being Black.

Similar to this, sometimes immigrant parents encourage their kids to marry someone white because they have perceived the power dynamic in America, and they know that *white* means *privilege*. They believe that having a white spouse will gain their kids social standing and help them to assimilate more fully into white American culture. In other words, white supremacy sometimes drives interracial marriage. If white is better, then marrying white is the next best thing to being white.

There are Black and Brown men who choose white partners so that they will have lighter kids; their brown skin has brought hardship, and they want to spare their kids from experiencing the same. When BIPOC men marry white women for these reasons, they usually leave the teaching of culture to their wives, and the children learn only white cultural values. You don't teach something you're trying to escape. Additionally, as these kids grow up, they see the stereotyped portrayals of people of color in the media, and they reject that part of themselves too.

Sometimes non-Asian men seek Asian women to marry because they perceive Asian women to be gentle, submissive, loyal, and/or hypersexualized. They believe the portrayal of Asian women in much of the media and seek out someone who fits that mold. Latina and Black women are also often oversexualized, and some men fetishize these women, attracted to them for selfish reasons. There are even books about dating and marrying BIPOC women, such as *How to Date and Marry the Right Black Woman: A White Man's Perspective* and *How to*

Meet, Date and Marry Beautiful Asian Women: It's Easier than You Think! These titles alone raise major red flags.

Lastly, some women rebel against a racist culture and become drawn to something or someone *different*. They are attracted to men outside of their race, but they don't grasp the emotional and psychological carnage caused by a racial caste system. They don't understand the deep cultural differences or the pain their husbands may be carrying, and they lack the tools to help alleviate that pain.

Of course, a lot of these can be true at the same time. You fell in love, or you fell in love plus you were trying to escape a painful past, or you fell in love plus you were drawn to a different ethnicity, or you fell in love plus you were rebelling against your parents' racism. We are human, which means our motives are never pure and they are often complex. But it's important to be honest with yourself so that you can help your kids in their identity development. If you married out of any kind of self-rejection, that needs to be healed, and if you married out of any kind of rebellion, that needs to be confronted. You may genuinely love your spouse and your marriage may otherwise stand on a solid foundation, but this part of it can wreak havoc in ways that will damage your kids' racial identity journey if you don't face it with honesty.

Years ago, an acquaintance made a comment about Black poverty being the result of a poor work ethic and single parent homes, and I called her on it. She didn't know that most Black people are not poor and that most Black people work very hard to support their families—just like white people. She had a Black husband and biracial kids, but she knew precious little about the Black experience. She didn't get along with her in-laws, and she lived in a mostly white community. Even though she fell in love with a Black man, she didn't have any Black friends and she never learned to appreciate Black culture. As a matter of fact, she was often annoyed by personality traits in her husband that had cultural roots.

Similarly, I once had a conversation with a single white woman who has a biracial son. She was raised in a small, white town, and one day, she met a young, handsome Black man, and the two had a short, fraught relationship. They didn't really love each other, nor did they understand each other; they both just wanted to *try something different.* The fruit of this infatuation was a biracial child whom she now raises with her parents in that same small town. Her parents not-so-secretly harbor racist views; their daughter's "predicament" only reinforces what they have always believed about Black men.

Unfortunately, her story is not unique.

One Sunday many years ago, a white woman approached me and asked for prayer; she wanted to be free from a toxic relationship. As we spoke, her own racism became evident. She said, "I can't believe I went out with him. I mean, he's BLACK— and you know BLACK men!" She spat out *BLACK* as if it were poison in her mouth. (Sometimes those with racist ideas feel free to express them to those of us with lighter skin because they consider us "different from the rest" and therefore "safe." This is one of many things biracial people have to navigate and disrupt.) The two conceived a child, and now her biracial son is being raised by a woman who clearly has little regard for Black people.

If you have biracial kids, you owe it to them to dig deep and uncover any latent racism hidden in your heart. Do you feel disdain for the way other people groups raise their children, think about time, express their emotions, or handle money? Do you think your culture is more in line with God's ideals? If you are married, do you value the way your spouse thinks, knowing that God placed her in your life to make you better and to provide wisdom and depth? As Paul writes, "The eye cannot say to the hand, 'I don't need you!' And the head cannot say to the feet, 'I don't need you!'" (1 Cor. 12:21 NIV). We need each other! No culture or people group possesses more of God's image than another. When you have a diverse family, you need diverse people in your life because on your own, you won't have all the wisdom it takes to raise your children.

David writes in Psalm 51, "Behold, you desire truth in the inward parts, and in the hidden part you will make me to know wisdom" (v. 6). Don't be afraid to look within and uncover pockets of racial bias hiding in your soul. Don't let shame keep you from honesty. You have BIPOC children now, so you owe it to them to interrogate your attitudes and assumptions and let God convict you of anything that does not line up with his heart toward all image bearers.

If you are no longer together with your child's other parent, what do you tell your kids about their father or mother? If your former partner, for example, was neglectful, do your kids subconsciously think this is because of his color? Have you forgiven him and learned to see and communicate his positive traits to your kids?

Similarly, are your kids' BIPOC grandparents less affluent than their white grandparents? If so, have you explained why it would have been nearly impossible for their BIPOC grands to earn and amass wealth, given the era in which they came of age?

Have you sought to educate yourself on the Black, or Asian or Hispanic experience in America? You can talk to your spouse about this, but do some of your own research too. Read James Baldwin and Toni Morrison, Gabriel García Márquez and Mario Vargas Llosa, Te-Ping Chen and Ocean Vuong. Don't depend on your spouse to provide all the history and culture. How wonderful it would be for your spouse to come home and find you reading a book about their homeland and history!

Also think about your family of origin. What did your parents intentionally or unintentionally teach you about racial or ethnic minority cultures? What words did they use, what assumptions did they have that may have settled into your soul? When Manuela, who is Mexican, told her family that she was going to marry a Black man, her sister-in-law commented, "Oh, you're going to have monkey babies!"[4] You may have weathered disapproval from family members when you chose to marry your spouse. I have a white friend who married a Chinese man, and her parents were so disapproving, they didn't even attend their wedding.

Now that you're married, perhaps that grandma, that uncle, that sister-in-law has come around and they have accepted your spouse and they love your kids. But what words do they use around your family? Do they use racial slurs? Do they prefer your kids who look less Asian, less Black, less Hispanic? Do they say your lighter daughter is more beautiful than your darker daughter? I have a Black friend who has a white husband, and when their first child was born, his grandmother refused to hold the baby. Do any of your family members harbor this level of racism? If so, protecting your kids from being wounded by these family members is your job.

What is on the television when you visit extended family? Do they watch racist media when your children are around? Do they think that your spouse is just an outlier, different from all the rest? Do they complain about "the infestation of illegal aliens" or the Chinese "taking over America"? Do they spit out comments about all the "animals" in the inner city or express disdain for race riots, not understanding or caring about the pain that sparked those riots in the first place? You may be accustomed to these comments and able to ignore them, but what about your kids? Do your kids hear Grandpa referring to Black or Brown people as criminals that need to be locked up? Do your white parents reminisce about the "good ol' days" around your teenagers? Your BIPOC teenagers are smart enough to put two and two together and realize that the "good ol' days" to which their grandparents are referring were oppressive to Black and Brown people.

Remember, your kids are watching and listening. If you simply roll your eyes and express mild irritation at these words, they will subconsciously feel that such attitudes are true or acceptable or just an annoyance. You may have to confront your parents for the sake of your children. You may have to swallow hard and tell your father, your uncle, your brother that, light or dark, your kids are equally beautiful and that you will not spend time together if they speak this way around your kids. As parents, one of our most important roles is protecting our kids, and this includes protecting them from racist family members.

On the other hand, if you are not white, what is your attitude toward white people? A Black friend with a white husband told me that at one time she found herself always speaking ill of white people, always calling them racist or bigoted or ignorant. And then one day her biracial children called her on it. She realized she was inadvertently sowing confusion into her children's hearts, subtly teaching them that white people were bad. If all white people were ignorant racists, what about Grandma, what about Dad, what about me? Is Dad just an exception? Should I not like or trust other white people? What about my peers at school or college or my future boss? Passing prejudice onto your kids will handicap them in every area of life.

Everything you think and feel, every belief you have, whether conscious or not, will be tacitly or not so tacitly communicated to your kids. Out of the abundance of the heart, the mouth speaks. What is in your heart about Black or Brown or Asian or white people?

If you have not healed from racial trauma, there is no way you can pass a healthy racial identity on to your kids. Our kids will inherit our brokenness, so we owe it to them to do the work to become whole, and wholeness often requires forgiving those who dishonored us. Who dishonored you because of your color? Who told you to go back home or treated you as if you were invisible?

It was not so long ago that Black men were called *boys*, and that Black people, young or old, had to step off curbs to let any white person pass. In your parents' or grandparents' generation, Hispanics were excluded from jobs, schools, and movie theaters and treated as a foreign underclass. Your parents may speak of the mass deportations that occurred in their lifetime, and this may engender fear or anger. Hispanic, Asian, and African Americans have all been targeted in hate crimes, which can make you feel scared and like it will never end. Despair is a real temptation for those who grew up looking over their shoulder and who *still* look over their shoulder now. Racial injustice sometimes feels like a metastasized disease.

If you are a Christian and you feel this way, talk to the Lord about it. The writer of Hebrews reassures, "This hope we have as an anchor of the soul, both sure and steadfast, and which enters the Presence behind the veil" (6:19). If you are a Christian, Jesus anchors us. If you are not a Christian, what anchors you and helps you to remain steadfast? If we just look at what's happening in the world, it can be easy to give into despair. But God can do what no man or woman can do. He will continue to inspire righteous change. He cares about racial and social justice and will continue to fight on behalf of the vulnerable.

Additionally, all of us should find a person to talk to. Especially since all the racial unrest of 2020, many therapists and counselors have learned how to talk to clients about racial wounds, and they know how to guide them to a place of wholeness.

Finally, if you are an immigrant yourself, what level of fear did you metabolize growing up in your homeland? Does this just make you want to forget and become as Americanized as quickly as possible? You cannot teach your child to be proud of his ethnic heritage if you are not proud of it yourself or if you want to pretend it doesn't exist. If you have closeted your racial or ethnic identity, it is time to open that door and discover *you* so that you can help your children discover themselves.

I am reminded of the prophet Jeremiah's lament: "Is there no balm in Gilead? Is there no physician there? Why then is there no healing for the wound of my people?" (Jer. 8:22 NIV). Jesus is the balm that can heal the Black and Brown soul. He may use a therapist, a pastor, or a close friend, but he wants to heal you so that you can love all of you and your kids can love all of themselves.

QUESTIONS TO PONDER

1. What motivated you to marry or date someone of a different race? If you are an adoptive parent, what motivated you to transracially adopt? Remember, motives are rarely pure, so don't be afraid to admit it if your motives were mixed.

2. Think about the words and attitudes that you express about different racial groups. What generalizations do you make? For example, do you say, "Black women are always so loud!" "Asians are so smart!" or "Those people in the inner city need to get their act together and work!" What kinds of things do you say when you let your guard down and talk about other people?

3. Has being Black or Brown ever felt like a burden? If so, in what ways? How does being BIPOC feel like a blessing and not a curse?

4. Have you talked with your partner about any racial trauma they might have experienced? How have you tried to be a safe place for them?

STEPS FOR APPLICATION

This time, our steps for application for you, not your kids

— Take some time and think about what you were taught about other cultures growing up. For example, I was told that West Indians were arrogant snobs, and now I'm married to one! What did you hear growing up?

— If you are white, think honestly about white supremacy. Do you believe that white people are globally wealthier than Black and Brown people because white culture is better? If you are married, do you harbor any feelings of superiority to your spouse or their extended family?

— What was your parents' or grandparents' attitude toward your spouse? Has it changed for the better over the course of your marriage?

— Does anyone in your extended family make racist comments when you and your family are around? What do you do about it?

— What BIPOC literature have you read? Consider reading something with your spouse or a BIPOC friend and then talking about it.

— Write down the most egregious racist experiences you have had. These can include having racial slurs hurled at you; being stopped unnecessarily by police while driving; feeling slighted by teachers, doctors, or others in authority; being denied a job or a promotion; suffering physical violence; and many others. How has that experience affected you? Have you forgiven the perpetrator? If not, now would be a good time to forgive them and ask God to heal your heart.

—What stories about racism did you hear growing up? Was your father or grandfather denied certain opportunities that affected your family? Did anyone experience racial violence? Hearing about racial oppression, even if you haven't experienced it, can cause a deep wound that needs to be healed. It's not that we shouldn't hear these stories; it's important to know what our parents have been through, but it can be difficult to know what to do with them. You may have to forgive those who wronged your family member and also deal with any fear or inferiority that has taken root in your heart.

—If you cannot get past these things on your own, consider seeing a counselor or therapist. I love what hip-hop artist Lecrae said about the therapist he found after experiencing so much racism: "It was this little white woman trying to understand me. She would say things like, 'Explain to me where you came from. Explain to me your history. Explain to me when you say this, what does that mean? So how did Michael Brown affect you? And what is your perspective?' And I was like, wow, you really want to know, and she would come back the next session with research and insight and thoughts and I was like, you really are learning from this process and some of her suggestions were very helpful and beneficial."[5]

—If you cannot afford a therapist or find one in your area, find an older, prayerful friend or pastor with whom you can be open and honest and share your experiences. Ask someone who is BIPOC themselves or who is humble enough to do the work to understand (as Lecrae described about his therapist). A white person can have insight but only if they are able to truly hear you and talk to you with empathy, wisdom, humility, and support. I realize this may be difficult; you may not be accustomed to digging deep, naming your feelings, and then trusting someone with what you find, but things hidden in darkness cannot heal. If you bring these painful experiences to the light, you will likely feel relieved and unburdened and better able to help your kids with their racial identity journey.

10

Be Honest with Your Kids

I figured I'd have to explain name-calling, have hard talks about language, navigate the waters when somebody's parents won't let my son take their daughter to the prom. . . . At no point . . . did I think I would have to teach my son how to stay alive.

—Robin Wells, white mom of Black adoptee[1]

Be honest with your kids about race and racism. One place to start is the racial history of your city. For example, over the years, we've sought to educate our kids about Rochester's grave history of racism. It's important for them to know why certain inequities exist where we live.

Rochester is the sixth poorest city in the country, and most of Rochester's poor are Black and Hispanic. It has an abysmal history of redlining, racial covenants, and job discrimination. It was also the perfect example of white flight. The suburban subdivisions that were built in the forties, fifties, and sixties were built for white families and white families alone. Families of color were not permitted to buy homes there, whether they could afford them or not. Realtors refused to show these subdivisions to them, and banks denied them mortgages. The federal government specifically denied Black and Brown people the low interest rates of FHA loans, yet these loans were the means through which millions of white families purchased homes, built equity, and entered the middle class. Some subdivisions boldly proclaimed on plaques: *No lot shall be occupied by a colored person. This restriction, however, shall not prevent the employment of a colored person as a domestic servant of the owner or occupant.*[2] The families who moved to these neighborhoods feared Black and Brown people and would tolerate seeing them only in a subservient role. They didn't want to live, learn, work, or worship anywhere near them. They left the city and took their property taxes with them, and Black and Brown people were denied the opportunity to join the middle class through home ownership.

Once white people were gone, businesses ceased investing in the city, property values decreased, schools fell into disrepair, and local funding plummeted. The only businesses that moved into these neighborhoods were liquor stores, corner stores, and check-cashing stores (with high fees). There were no banks, no libraries, no supermarkets, no restaurants, no supply shops, no bookstores, no coffee shops.

While Rochester's suburbs are majority white, and their schools boast some of the highest rankings in the nation, the city is largely BIPOC, and its schools rank among the worst in the nation. Unlike the professional Black populations in Atlanta, Washington DC, Houston, and other cities, the professional Black population in Rochester is very small, and when white Rochesterians see Black people, many assume poverty—and crime.

We've explained all this to our kids. Kids see disparity, and if they don't understand the reason for it, they will likely draw wrong conclusions such as, "Well, white people must be better!" Or, "What's wrong with Black and Brown people?" Do obvious disparities exist in your community? Do you pass through (or avoid) an area which is mostly BIPOC? Are white neighborhoods nicer? If so, have you researched the reasons and explained them to your kids?

Our entire region, western New York, also has a majority white population. Many of the whites who live here attended mostly white schools and white colleges where they made white friendships and then settled down with their white families in white neighborhoods. They've lived their whole lives hearing terrifying stories of all the crime "downstate," that is, in New York City, *where the minorities live*, and they are quite content to live tucked far away from anyone Brown.

This reality smacked Marvin and me in the face when we first moved here. We like some things about Rochester, but we don't like the stares we often receive when we walk into a suburban restaurant. We also don't like the effort we have to put forth making sure our sons grow up with a healthy racial identity.

Having grown up in a Black nation, Marvin didn't know what racism was until he left to attend college in London. Growing up, his soul was never damaged by white supremacy. His friends were Black, his teachers were Black, his pediatrician was Black. The principals in his schools were Black, and the prime minister was Black. The criminals were Black, and the police officers who arrested them were Black. It never entered his mind that melanin made him less: less intelligent, less safe, less good. He didn't have any deficits from failing to learn about famous Black people in school; the majority of people he learned about in school were Black. He grew up with an uncomplicated national pride and never experienced the confusion of *two-ness*. When he moved to England, however, he did have to figure out how to *stay* Jamaican and not slowly lose himself trying to assimilate with white peers. He found the West Indian neighborhoods: the people, the food, the barber shops, the vibe. He learned how to deal with police stopping him and the racist assumptions of classmates and professors.

These lessons, along with the things I learned in my college and post-college years, would prove crucial in raising Black sons not only in America but in a predominately white community. We moved to the suburbs because we heard troubling statistics about the city schools, but living in a mostly white district comes with other negative realities. While BIPOC attending city schools deal with systemic racism, BIPOC attending suburban schools deal with relational racism. I honestly don't know which one is worse; both are heavy burdens to bear.

Perhaps because of your community or country of origin you were very grounded in your racial or ethnic identity, but now your kids are growing up with a different reality. You grew up with all the benefits that come with being in the majority, but your kids are very much in the minority. It's important to realize that your kids need support that you didn't need.

The Importance of Advocacy

Over the years we've learned of birthday parties of alleged friends that my boys were not invited to and neighborhood social events from which our family was excluded. My boys have felt the weight of loneliness and have wondered if a teacher's lack of regard had anything to do with their color. Sending an email or calling the school has become routine as I question a teacher's response to one of my son's actions; I ask questions; I poke and prod, trying to determine if racial bias played any role. It has been well documented that in schools across the nation, BIPOC kids make up the majority of students corrected, suspended, expelled, or sent to the principal's office for the same behaviors as white students, who receive only a slap on the wrist. Listening, watching, asking, advocating for our sons: these are regular parts of our family life.

If you are white, perhaps this kind of advocacy is new to you. Your parents may have attended parent-teacher conferences, but they didn't feel the need to check for bias; they didn't worry about this level of unfairness. But if your kids don't look white, it's important for you to realize they likely need more advocacy than you did. If they come home and tell you that a teacher doesn't like them or treats them differently from the other kids, take note. Your child may be misinterpreting things, or she may be sensing something that's true. Don't be dismissive, but prod, ask questions, and, if need be, have a respectful conversation with the teacher to try to determine what's going on.

I tend to be a people-pleaser, but when it comes to my sons, I really could care less if teachers find me annoying. They know Marvin and I are deeply invested; our eyes are wide open, and we will question anything that feels suspect.

I'd rather be wrong than find out my kids were struggling in a hostile school environment.

Sometimes one of our boys asks if something was racist.

"Do you think my teacher yelled at me because I'm Black?"

"Not necessarily. Were you being annoying or disrespectful?"

"No."

"Well, does she yell at other students sometimes too?"

"Sometimes. Hmmm. Maybe she was just having a bad day."

"That's very possible. Let me know if it happens again."

I don't want my kids to be hyper-focused on racism, so I give the benefit of the doubt if I can, but I watch and keep track, and if things don't improve, I make a phone call. I'm trying to be honest with my kids and teach them discernment without making them fearful or resentful.

We make a point of meeting their teachers at the beginning of each school year to shake their hands and let them know that we are here, attentive and watching. I also ask about the books they'll be reading, the history they'll be learning. How many people of color will they learn about and how will slavery and the Civil War be taught? I ask if they'll learn about precolonial Africa: about its wealth and greatness. Perhaps you can ask if your kids will be reading any Asian or Latinx authors, if they will learn the history of anti-immigrant policies and sentiment in the United States, and the significant contributions of immigrants in American history. If such things aren't part of the curricula, you can advocate for change and, in the meantime, borrow books from the library about them for your kids to read at home.

As parents, we should never depend on schools to teach our kids everything they need to know about their ethnic heritage. Part of their identity development will be learning about talented people of color, and schools don't teach this enough. Indeed, some schools have removed Black and Brown stories from curricula and libraries because these stories often include ugly accounts of racial oppression. These districts worry that such narratives will make all kids less patriotic and white children uncomfortable. Unfortunately, these concerns take precedence over historical truth-telling. This makes it even more critical that we provide books about our kids' Mixed heritage so that they will understand what their forefathers overcame and what they accomplished despite great opposition.

We've also had to advocate for our boys at the doctor's office. When one of our boys was little, he started to see a specialist for an issue, and when he and my husband walked in for the first time, my husband felt instant disregard. The doctor wouldn't look him in the eye; he was dismissive and patronizing. But when Marvin mentioned where he went to university and what he did for a living, the doctor's attitude completely changed. He became more personable, more attentive to my son, and more respectful of Marvin. Marvin hates talking about his credentials, but he will do it if it means fair and kind treatment for our family.

When our kids were younger, I might have a conversation with a teacher without my kids knowing, but now that they are teenagers, we tell them more about these kinds of dynamics. We tell them that we're advocating for them, that we're watchful and listening. They tease me about being scary: "Don't mess with my mom!" They know I'm professional and respectful, but they also know that I will make the phone call and have a pointed conversation if necessary.

Talking about Racism Protects Our Kids

As parents, we have a powerful drive to protect our children, and sometimes we may be reluctant to talk about the realities of racial bias because we want to insulate them from that pain. We don't want them to feel as if there's something wrong with them, and we don't want to scare them that one day they may not be liked or, worse, suffer harm, simply because of the way they look. But withholding conversation about racism is similar to withholding conversation about sex: *Maybe if I don't talk about it, they won't do it. Or in this case, maybe if I don't talk about it, it won't happen.* We know that the former is false, and so is the latter.

BE HONEST WITH YOUR KIDS

Dr. Juliana Chen, a child and adolescent psychiatrist at Mass General Brigham in Boston, said that it's important to ask your kids certain questions: What have you heard? What do you worry about? What's school like for you and your friends? Has anything like this ever happened to you or someone you know? She said that sometimes when kids experience racism, they stop speaking up or even showing up in school. They get the message that they are different, *other*, unwelcome, and unwanted, and they may struggle with poor sleep or depression. "We think we're protecting our kids by not talking about racist incidents. . . . But actually, not talking about it is not helping."[3]

It is a lack of candor about racism that sets kids up for a big fall. If they have no idea they might be disrespected because of their color, they will be devastated if it happens. I'm reminded about the story of the white adoptive parents who didn't talk about racism with their adopted Black son, Alex. They lived in a middle-class, white neighborhood, and the parents never thought or talked about racial profiling. And then Alex started driving. One day a police officer pulled him over and asked him to open his trunk, but when Alex asked for a warrant, four officers proceeded to beat him so severely that he wound up with forty-six stitches and a traumatic brain injury. He thought he was going to die. His parents' ignorance and reticence about racism didn't protect him that night. In his mind, he could ask the officer that very rational question about the warrant because it was his legal right to do so. But we have to teach our kids that though it might be their legal right to request something, it may not be wise to demand it. He should have known the risk of standing up to the officer. Years later, Alex received an $800,000 settlement from the City of Denver; the police officers were fired but never charged, and his parents regret their silence.[4]

Writer Heidi Shin started talking to her seven-year-old daughter about racism when a girl from their neighborhood stopped playing with her because of the "Chinese virus." That's when she started reading books with Asian-American heroines by authors like Grace Lin and Min Jin Lee. She pointed out these characters' stories were like her family story, and her daughter at one point jumped up from the couch and shouted, "She likes to eat dduk guk"—Korean rice cake soup—"like me!"[5]

Before her daughter's experience with the neighborhood girl, Shin took the assimilation approach, desiring her daughter to blend in and be like the other children. But after the "Chinese virus" comment, she realized her daughter does not look white and will never be white, and so she should take pride in her Asian heritage. It took her daughter's experience with racism to drive home the fact that it was time to teach her daughter about her heritage; if she was going to experience the pain of anti-Asian hate, she needed to experience the pride of being Asian even more.

Kids start to develop a sense of racial identity by the time they are three or four, and then, once they start school, they hear about racism and begin to experience it themselves (like my son in the duck, duck, goose game). Parents, loving your kids means keeping them safe, and part of keeping them safe means talking to them about racism.

Jesus said to his disciples, "Behold, I am sending you out as sheep in the midst of wolves; so be as wary as serpents, and as innocent as doves" (Matt. 10:16 NASB). As parents, we teach our kids how to live and move in this world with wisdom. Sadly, part of wisdom is knowing how to respond in racist situations. They have to have eyes wide open, being wary, not naive. But we also want them to retain their innocence and not become fearful, resentful, or suspicious. So, we talk to them, ask good questions, and listen attentively to what they say. We teach them discernment, how to know good from evil and how to respond if they encounter evil. We also often point out kindness so that they realize most people with whom they interact are good people; this way they won't become jaded, always assuming the worst. Teach them to assume the best, but plan for the worst.

"The Talk" for Boys

From the time they were young, we have had hard conversations with our boys, trying to equip them to live and thrive in a country that still harbors assumptions that Black men are dangerous, less moral, and less intelligent. These conversations have been termed "The Talk," and parents of Black children have these conversations with their children in one form or another all over the country. Unless your children look white, you should have some version of "The Talk" with them too.

For Black and Brown boys, this conversation centers around not looking suspicious, avoiding being profiled, responding calmly to police, being as unintimidating as possible. As Kathryn D'Angelo, white mother of a Black adoptee, wrote, "Our world does not give our son the privilege of acting like us, and moreover, it places on him the burden of managing how others feel about him."[6] It is difficult but necessary to teach our kids about this burden. We started early with our boys and add more caveats the older they get:

— When you're walking, riding your bike, or someday driving and a police officer stops you, keep your hands where he can see them. Don't reach for your phone. Don't talk back. Don't raise your voice. Don't become defensive. Stay calm. Agree with him, even if he's wrong. Don't make him nervous.

— You may not play with BB guns, paintball guns, air soft guns, or any other gun that is not brightly colored with ammunition made of orange foam.

— Always ask for a bag in the store. Don't walk out with an item not in a bag. The shopkeeper may think you're stealing it.

WHAT ABOUT THE CHILDREN?

—Don't wear the hood up on your hoodie, even if you're cold. Our boys know about Trayvon Martin. They know that hooded Black boys are often viewed as suspicious.

—Always look neat and clean at school or in public (no sweats or stained clothes, no pajamas outside). Sloppy clothes increase the likelihood of being stereotyped or profiled.

We are also aware that Black boys sometimes look older than they are; they often lose their baby cheeks and develop muscles and facial hair sooner than some white boys.[7] Sadly, this can exacerbate the tendency to profile Black boys, even though they are not yet men. One of our sons wanted to grow a beard recently and we said no. We want him to look as young as possible for as long as possible.

We have told our sons again and again that if one day a police officer stops them and dishonors them, this does not reflect on them but reveals deeply entrenched racial bias. We want them to be able to swallow hard, walk away, and deal with the offense not in the street but in a courtroom, a therapist's room, or a living room—so that they will live.

When they start dating, it will be important for them to know that one of the stereotypes of Black and Brown men is that they are oversexed and predatory toward women. All boys should be taught to respect women, to back off if their girlfriend says no, and to avoid being alone with girls they don't really know. But episodes of white girls falsely accusing Black and Brown boys of rape have been around for a long time, and this has led to countless convictions and even lynchings of BIPOC boys and men. Black and Brown boys are more vulnerable to being misunderstood and falsely accused of misdeeds. People often think about warning their daughters to be on guard and not overly trusting until they really know a boy. But BIPOC boys need the same lesson, especially if they're dating white girls.

"The Talk" is crucial for these boys because men of color have been feared for a long time. As a matter of fact, it was once believed that Black people were Black because they were complicit with the devil. Such ideas justified bondage, then segregation, and then police brutality. Black men were allegedly naturally inclined to violence and sexual conquest. The movie *The Birth of a Nation*, which was first screened at Woodrow Wilson's White House in 1920, was a box office hit and one of the highest grossing films of all time. It depicted a brutish Black man stalking an innocent white woman until she reached the edge of a cliff and flung herself over to her death, all to escape being ravished by this dark, yellow-eyed brute. In the movie, white men dressed in white sheets and hoods rode white horses protecting white women's virtue and the old way of life. The message: Black men need to be kept separate and in check, even through violence, or else they will plunder everything and everyone in their path.

Today, the belief persists that Black men are inherently more dangerous than white men, and this lies at the root of so many police shootings. Somehow, deep within the American psyche, this ancient myth still exists. It helps white people feel superior and justifies the use of force: if you're a Black male, you're more likely malevolent, and you should be given no benefit of the doubt, no second chance.

"He looks like a really bad dude," said a police officer as he hovered in a helicopter above Terence Crutcher before another officer ended Crutcher's life.[8] How exactly did Crutcher look *really bad*? Was he waving a gun, a grenade, a knife? Was he spewing out threats and profanity? No. He was only Black. How exactly did twelve-year-old Tamir Rice look dangerous? In every corner of the globe, boys (and some girls) play with toy guns. Why was Tamir not permitted to be a kid and play with a toy gun without triggering fear, which led to a white police officer, Timothy Loehmann, triggering his gun and ending young Tamir's life? In response to losing her son, Tamir's mother, Samaria Rice, wrote the poignant *Tamir Rice Safety Handbook*, providing guidance for African American youth on how to deal with confrontations with police.[9] How tragic that a grieving mother felt the need to write such a book. In our culture, Black people, even Black children, carry the burden of putting white people at ease.

Mexican men also have been portrayed as lazy, dirty, menacing criminals. Presidents and politicians suggest they are rapists. Hispanic men in general are often depicted in the media as drug dealers: cruel and merciless. This stokes anti-immigrant sentiment and makes Hispanic men vulnerable to profiling.

Especially since 9/11, anyone who looks Middle Eastern is suspect. Hollywood represents Middle Eastern men as barbaric and violent. They are cruel to women, insidious, and secretly hedonistic. In production after production, even Middle Eastern men who appear to be patriotic are covertly helping jihadist radicals, their love for America a mere show to cover their duplicity. Hollywood predisposes us to be afraid and distrustful of men from this part of the world.

The truth, of course, is that Black and Brown men have no more proclivity for criminal behavior than white men, and yet we are regularly fed this very idea. If your kids are partly Black or partly Hispanic or partly Middle Eastern, they may experience this kind of ignorant distrust from kids, teachers, police officers, and TSA workers, and it is better for them if you talk about it, in age-appropriate ways, so that they are not devastated if it happens.

It is often fathers of color who talk to their sons about staying safe with the police, but if Dad is white, he may be tempted to downplay this possibility because neither he nor anyone in his extended family has ever experienced such a thing. He may think that only troublemakers get stopped and that if your son acts right, he'll be fine. Sadly, this is not true. If Dad is white, this is where humility comes to play again. Dad, you need to be humble enough to ask for help. You might invite a Black male friend over or ask someone from your wife's extended family to chime in with wisdom. You can read about racial profiling, but it's important for

BE HONEST WITH YOUR KIDS 139

your sons to hear from someone with firsthand experience. Know your limits and don't be afraid to ask for help. Also, don't dismiss your wife's concerns about this. The men in her extended family may have gone through this, and now she fears her sons will too. Unfortunately, this is not an irrational fear. Take her concerns seriously and talk together about how to teach your sons to be safe.

In his book *Whistling Vivaldi: How Stereotypes Affect Us and What We Can Do*, social psychologist Claude Steele tells the story of a Black University of Chicago student. This student noticed white people on the street drawing back and walking the long way around him and white women clutching their purses when he passed. But then one day, he happened to be whistling part of Vivaldi's *The Four Seasons* as he walked, and he noticed a complete change in how white people responded to him. Now they nodded, and some even said, "Hi." When he whistled Vivaldi, white people no longer responded to him in fear. They saw him as a young university student. He disarmed them by whistling a familiar tune considered sophisticated, and so he took up this practice to keep himself safe.[10]

Parents, I'm not suggesting that you teach your boys to whistle *The Four Seasons*, but I am suggesting that you teach them strategies for living and moving in a world that may see them as dangerous. Giving boys "The Talk" is part of this.

"The Talk" for Girls

"The Talk" for girls covers some of the same points as "The Talk" for boys, but it also includes more about sexual stereotypes. BIPOC girls have been falsely accused of theft and other nefarious deeds, but "The Talk" for them also emphasizes how they may be perceived sexually.

As I entered my teens, I began to receive more attention from older white men, but it was purely sexual. These men hinted at sex or outright asked for it, no doubt because they found me exotic. They boldly propositioned me, an underaged girl, but thankfully I said no. Their advances scared me as they seemed predatory, and I walked out of many situations. Your Mixed-race daughter should know that she, too, may be considered exotic, and exotic will target her for sexual conquest. Just as there is a Dangerous Black Man Myth, there is a Hypersexual Black, Hispanic, and Asian Woman Myth. All are often cast as seductive, mysterious, alluring. They are trophy wives and not very intelligent. Their accents make them cute and desirable but not to be taken seriously.

In some contexts, your Mixed daughter may not stand out. A biracial friend did not stand out because she grew up in a neighborhood heavily populated by Latin American immigrants; most of the people on her block and the surrounding blocks were some shade of brown. If you don't live in this kind of community, though, tan will be different, and different might be targeted for negative sexual attention. Teach your daughter what selfish sexual interest looks like and that she shouldn't be flattered by it.

Mixed-race girls need enough self-respect and confidence so that they don't succumb to this ill-intended attention. If they are too desperate to fit in, they will undersell themselves and suffer tremendous consequences. Your daughter's ambiguous-seeming ethnicity may make her intriguing to some men, but this doesn't mean that those men are interested in her for who she is. Rather, they see her as more of a fetish to be used rather than a woman to be loved.

I want to discuss one last, myth here: the Myth of the Tragic Mulatto. The tragic mulatto is a woman born of a white enslaver and a Black slave. She is light enough to pass for white, so she rejects her Black family, ultimately gains her freedom, and joins the white world. She even takes a white lover. In the end, however, she is discovered to be Mixed race, her lover abandons her, and the white world spurns her. She wanders in a no-man's-land of rejection until she finally takes her life.

Depressing, I know, but the myth is illustrative of several lies. Lie #1: This woman can be happy only if she denies her Black heritage and pretends to be white. Lie #2: If that pretense is ever discovered, the only reasonable recourse is suicide. And Lie #3: If she ever fully embraced all of her ethnic details, no one would ever love her. Parents, teach your daughters that these lies come from the enemy of their souls. Let them know they are thoroughly beautiful and help them to be so grounded in your love and in God's love that they have enough self-respect and dignity to have no interest in someone who sees them purely as an exotic land to be conquered.

I have found that white women can sometimes be naive about the fascination some white men have with women of color. I want to warn you that your daughter may receive attention you did not receive at her age because you were not considered exotic. Also, like BIPOC boys, BIPOC girls sometimes physically develop sooner than white girls. They lose their little girl look and become curvier and womanlier at a younger age, so that men of all colors think they are older than they are. All of which is to say, your Mixed-race daughter may need more of your protection than you needed from your parents. Just keep your eyes open; notice if men swarm around her like bees to honey and help her to stay grounded and wise. Also help her to choose clothes that are appropriate for her age and body type. Let her know it would be better for her not to date until she's older than to date prematurely and have her heart broken by someone who wants to use her.

A good man will not have *a thing* for ethnic women, but will be open and kind, willing to humbly learn about your daughter's cultural heritage. He will be brave, knowing he is embarking on unfamiliar territory but willing because he truly cares for your daughter.

QUESTIONS TO PONDER

1. Did you grow up in a community very different from the community in which you now live with your family? How might those differences affect your children?

2. Have you and your spouse discussed "The Talk"? What will that look like and when will you start having it? Please remember this is not a one-and-done conversation. It will be ongoing as you add different components the older your children become.

3. Have you talked to your kids about why white neighborhoods often look nicer than BIPOC neighborhoods? Also, how much does your family stand out in your neighborhood and school district? Have you ever had to advocate for your kids at school or at the doctor's office because you sensed negative racial bias?

4. White dads, have you considered that your sons may have a different relationship with the police than you had? Do you have close friends who are men of color who can help teach your sons about how to stay safe during encounters with the police or other authority figures?

5. White moms, have you considered that your daughters will likely have a different experience navigating the waters of boys and dating than you had? In what ways are you teaching your daughters how to stay safe around men who see them as exotic?

STEPS FOR APPLICATION

Toddlers and Preschoolers

— If you are a Christian, teach Bible stories about injustice and bias. For example, talk to them about Peter's reluctance to teach Gentiles and the parable of the Good Samaritan. Let them know that even today, people may treat others badly because of differences like skin color, and this is wrong and mean.

— Teach your kids why your family may look different from other families. In some families, moms and dads have the same skin color, but in your family, mom and dad have different skin colors and they are a wonderful combination of both.

Elementary School

— Begin to read books and watch movies that show people being mistreated because of their race. Ask probing questions like, "Why do you think that boy teased that girl about her hair?" Help your kids to see how wrong that is and ask them what they'd do if it happened to them. Read books about Harriet Tubman or Li Keng Wong, a seven-year-old detained at Angel Island Immigration Station in the 1930s. Talk about how unjust it was that people were enslaved or detained just because of the color of their skin and how brave they were in the face of that.

— Tell them that even today people are sometimes treated badly because of their race. Let them know it is foolish to think someone is bad just because of the color of their skin. It is also sin: God doesn't approve of it, but rather he made us all in his image and he expects us to treat everyone with dignity and worth.

WHAT ABOUT THE CHILDREN?

—Ask them if someone has ever teased them about their hair, their eyes, their color. Ask them what they worry about and what school is like for them and their friends.

Tweens and Teens

—Talk about difficult things in the news, past and present. Tell them that Black and Hispanic Americans are killed by police far more often than white Americans.[11] This is not because Black and Hispanic people commit more crimes, but because they are shown less mercy in tense situations. Let them know that this is not just; God shows no partiality.

—Talk about Scriptures about injustice such as Deuteronomy 10:17; Proverbs 20:23; Romans 9:14; and James 2:1–13. These and other passages make it clear that showing partiality and treating a person, or a people group, better or worse than another is not God's way.

—Provide practical wisdom to help keep them safe. Some people of color make sure their kids dress in a certain way to help curtail profiling (like not wearing hoods or saggy pants). Some resist that, wanting their kids to be able to express themselves the way other kids do. Decide with your spouse which way suits your family.

—Be aware of how those around them react toward them. A biracial friend talked about the difference between the way she and her siblings were treated with their white mom versus when they were with their Black dad. She said that when they went to the store with their mom, things usually went fine, but when they went with their dad, they were followed by security guards and treated with suspicion. Have your eyes wide open to this kind of dynamic and let your kids know this is rooted in racism and is no reflection on their parent or on them.

— Teach your kids to always come to you if they believe they are being treated unfairly at school or anywhere else. Teach them resilience and courage: sometimes in life they will have to let go and move on, but other times, a confrontation or candid conversation is warranted.

— Help your kids to be secure and confident. Tell them often how beautiful they are, both inside and out. If girls hear this from their parents and other family members, they will be less likely to crave hearing it from men. And if boys hear this often enough, they will know that the Myth of the Dangerous Black Man is certainly nothing more than a myth.

VALUE V

Exploration

11

Dating, Marriage, and Beyond

Ultimately, it is a mixed person's prerogative to be fluid in their identity, for them to sometimes hold one, or both, and for that to change over time.

—Ronald R. Sundstrom[1]

The last value we will discuss is *exploration*, that is, giving your kids the room to explore their racial identity and being aware that racial identity is dynamic; it may change in different seasons of their lives or even in different circumstances. Also, as they enter adolescence, the way they identify will likely affect whom they want to date and, one day, marry.

Because I grew up around so many white people, I adopted white beauty standards for myself (which were impossible to meet) and white beauty standards for boys. In other words, once I started liking boys, I wanted to date only white boys. I was so accustomed to being around people with Eurocentric features that people who didn't have those features weren't attractive to me. Just like there were no magazines with pictures of beautiful Black women laying around my house, there were no magazines with handsome Black men either. *Tiger Beat*, the ultimate magazine for teenage girls, featured only John Travolta, Shaun Cassidy, Leif Garrett, and the like: no Black, Asian, or Hispanic men.

Added to that, my dad's depression led to many negative things, including obesity. Food was his substance of choice and then sleeping to forget. I wasn't proud of my dad, and, on a subliminal level, that resulted in me being turned off of Black men. My dad was usually unemployed, and at home he was often short-tempered and sullen (though in social situations he lit up and came alive). The atmosphere in our house was often tense and unhappy, mostly because of his failure to provide and my mom's reaction to it.

When you add to that the unkindness of my Black peers and Black stereotypes in the media juxtaposed with the shiny exterior of the white world, I completely gravitated to it and the boys in it. But when those white boys rejected me, my self-esteem faltered even more.

Dear parents, if your kids are beginning to have romantic interests, to whom are they attracted? Whom do they have crushes on? Whom do they consider beautiful? One of the things that reveals deficits in racial identity development is dating. I'm not suggesting that Mixed-race people should date only someone who has the same BIPOC heritage as they: that your biracial Asian kids, for example, should date only Asians. However, if they are categorically unattracted to Asians, this may indicate a dissociation with their Asian heritage. Do they see themselves as white or wish they were white and ultimately want to date only white? When you point out Asian men, do they crinkle their nose and say, "No way!" Do your daughters believe the stereotype that Asian men are unmanly, timid, or nerdy? Similarly, do your kids associate Black or Hispanic men with pejoratives and have no interest in dating them? Asian-Canadian author Katharine Chan writes,

> As I entered high school, I started watching more Hollywood movies and television shows. From "She's All That," "Can't Hardly Wait" to "Notting Hill," I was obsessed with '90s rom-coms. I would put myself in the female lead's position, dream of getting that makeover, catching the attention of the hot guy, and living happily ever after. My dreams of marrying Aaron Kwok were replaced by the tall, dark, and handsome [white] Prince Charming that popped on my screen every weekend.[2]

DATING, MARRIAGE, AND BEYOND

She says that while attending a predominately white school, she and her Asian friends kept hoping a white guy would ask them out: "My Asian friends and I had secret crushes on them, always hoping they could see our olive faces in the crowd of tall, popular, and athletic white girls." Yet they went unseen by these boys. Chan's gravitation to white men ceased when she went to college and became surrounded by more Asian men. As she got to know some of them, she realized there was a lot of commonalities in their upbringing and values; her priorities changed, and she ultimately married one of them. My story is similar.

I never had a lot of boyfriends, but with few exceptions the ones I had were white. I liked white guys and always hoped they would like me back, and some did. These relationships, though, never lasted long, and race was usually a factor in a breakup. Some admitted that introducing me to their parents would be problematic, and some simply withdrew after a short time with little explanation. After the initial disappointment of breaking up, I always felt relieved, like I couldn't believe I went out with them in the first place. Each one had his own deep issues, and each time I felt as if I had dodged a bullet.

Three things happened during my single years that led to my choice to marry someone Black. First, I realized that dysfunction was no respecter of color. Yes, my father had a lot of problems, but so did the white men I dated. (I remember going out with one guy who had very little ambition; though in his thirties, he seemed content with a job he barely liked and had no plans of doing anything more. After we broke up, I thought, "OK, so white men can be underachievers too!") Second, I fell in love with Black people and Black culture, and third, I forgave my dad.

Over time, I realized that my dad simply, desperately wanted to prove himself, and he didn't grasp the importance of just stepping up and providing, even if it meant doing something he didn't enjoy. I eventually cut my father some slack and realized that he had grown up in a time when, at every turn, Black men were told they were subhuman. His failed business ventures put stress on our family; he made many poor choices, but he loved us, and it saddens me that he died likely feeling like a failure.

Forgiving my dad set me free to date Black men. Not only was I suddenly drawn to Black men, but I realized I wanted someone who would understand me and my family, especially my dad. Once I stopped judging my father, I desired a life partner who would also be generous toward him and understand the profound struggles that left scarred so many of the Black men who came of age during the time in which he did.

The more I identified as Black, the more I hung out with Black folks, and the more I experienced Black excellence, the more attracted to Black men I became. I spent a lot of time explaining racism to white people, and I realized I didn't want to have to explain it to my future spouse too. I wanted someone who knew the reality of it, faced it himself, and had the strength to rise above any resentment it produced. I also wanted someone who carried within himself the richness of blackness. I realized that if I married someone white, I would likely bend and twist to join his world. I spent my adolescence doing that, and I didn't want to run the risk of doing it again.

Chan articulates so well, "Being surrounded by more Asian males, I realized we had a lot in common. From values, beliefs, and the conditions we grew up with, there was a lot that connected us aside from the shape of our eyes. . . . I preferred to date Chinese men; I found it easier to connect on a cultural, mental, and emotional level."[3]

I began to find the same thing about Black men. Though I was culturally white in many ways, I was also Black in other ways. My upbringing was different from that of my white friends, and much of that was because I had a Black father and Black grandparents. Their imprint was indelibly, inextricably on my life, and I was proud of it.

One Sunday, a tall, dark Jamaican walked into my church, came up to me after the service, and shook my hand. Marvin's parents were part of the Windrush generation, that is, West Indians who emigrated to Britain to help rebuild cities like London after WWII. Marvin was born there, but grew up

DATING, MARRIAGE, AND BEYOND   153

in Jamaica and then returned to England for college. He did his postdoctoral work in Holland and then accepted a faculty position at Dartmouth. Then he decided he needed to find a church. Who would have thought that two people from such divergent places would converge in Hanover, New Hampshire? But we did meet, and we became friends, dated, and fell in love. Over the years, we have found that the common thread of the Black experience helps us to understand each other and our families on a deep level. Marvin is very aware of the culturally white part of me, and he loves and accepts that too. He doesn't try to make me blacker, though he does sometimes tease me about my (lack of) dancing skills, and he was pleasantly surprised that I recognized Nina Simone's voice on a record he was playing.

I've also often mused that Marvin has so many of my father's positive traits and none of his negative ones. He has the same easy laugh, the same generous spirit, the same winsome way around people. The same smile that lights up a room and draws you in. He even gives me the same lectures as my dad, "Just be yourself, Nicole, and don't worry so much about what people think!" But Marvin had no racial trauma to overcome, and he grew up hearing again and again that education was the way out of poverty; he was determined to achieve. By the time he moved to England, he was so grounded in himself that racist comments from professors and peers left him not only undeterred but also more resolved than ever to succeed.

I'm so glad my racial identity journey led me to Marvin.

Whom your kids choose to date can expose holes in racial identity development in some and racism in others.

My friend's Black daughter had a disconcerting conversation with a Black male classmate. He told her that he dates only white girls. This young man was adopted by a white family and has not been taught the beauty of blackness. He lives in a white world, has grown accustomed to white features, and has absorbed white beauty standards. The young lady put him in his place and said, "Have you looked at yourself in the mirror lately? You do know that you are Black, don't you? To reject Black women is to reject yourself!"

One Black college student spoke about her experiences with online dating. She described her interactions on dating apps as "weird" and "uncomfortable": "Whenever I'd match with a white guy, he would always have to acknowledge the fact that I was Black and that he's never been with a Black girl. . . . It makes me feel like a conquest novelty or something, like you don't have the respect or awareness to interact with me as a human being."[4]

Another woman shared the same experience, "I don't know if they're just treating me as an exotic thing that they want to try out because they've never dated a Black girl before, but I'm not here to be a social experiment for you."[5] Dating can be hard regardless of racial difference, but when race gets added to the mix, it can make things even more difficult. No one wants to be objectified or rejected because of the color of their skin.

Research done by dating apps determined that users place a premium on dating within their race. The only groups that are not categorically discriminated against are white men and Asian women. "People of color open to dating outside their own race must resign themselves to the fact that large portions of the dating pool, white or otherwise, exist outside the sphere of possibility."[6]

On her podcast *Archetypes*, Meghan Markle talked about becoming aware of race when she started dating Prince Harry, "I mean, if there's any time in my life that it's been more focused on my race, it's only once I started dating my husband. Then I started to understand what it was like to be treated like a Black woman. . . . Because up until then, I had been treated like a mixed woman. And things really shifted."[7]

Your kids may have moved through life enjoying some level of privilege because of their lighter skin, but when they start thinking about dating, race becomes more amplified, whether they date royalty or not.

As I said, the answer isn't to date only BIPOC but rather to find someone who is humble and ready to learn. Your children should date people who are interested in every part of them, including their ethnic heritage. Anyone they date should

DATING, MARRIAGE, AND BEYOND 155

be curious, generous, and open. Their love interests should ask questions, seeking to understand, withholding judgment, and being appreciative of difference. They should love your children's physical traits, without being overly fixated on them. The white men that I dated tried to be color-blind, and when that proved impossible, they faded out of my life. Teach your children to avoid those who have adopted a color-blind mentality. As we discussed in the beginning of this book, color is not shameful or something to circumvent. Color is indicative of heritage and is an unmovable part of their identity, and only someone who sees it, loves it, and wants to understand everything that comes with it will be a suitable match for your kid.

My Puerto Rican friend, Sophia, has a white husband. She said that one of the things she found attractive about him was his knowledge of all kinds of history and his willingness to learn more. Even though he grew up in a small, white town, he is broad-minded and appreciates all kinds of people. He cooks Puerto Rican food and dances salsa and merengue; even though he doesn't particularly like to dance, he learned these because Sophia loves to dance at social gatherings. This was a big part of him embracing her culture. He also supports her in teaching Puerto Rican values to their kids.

Sophia misses Puerto Rico. Her grandparents grew up farming on the island's interior, and to pass the time after hours, they'd play music, which was an amalgamation of African, Taino, and Spanish sounds. They migrated to the United States for a better life and slowly sent for more and more family members so that their community here in Rochester grew to be rich in extended family and culture. Sophia sees the value of the simpler life her grandparents left and prefers many aspects of that over American busyness and isolation. She hopes that her daughters won't move too far away so that they, too, can enjoy having family nearby. Her husband understands all of that. Part of what makes a good marriage is being with someone who can be trusted with our heart's longings and musings, someone who will understand we may have left culture behind that we miss and someone who will help figure out a way to have more of that culture in our lives.

Biracial Korean Tasha Jun also has a white husband, and she shares that when they were first married, she worried that she would be too Asian for them to stay together. But over time, she saw that he didn't "have a thing for Asians" and that he wasn't adventurous for the sake of adventure, rather "he was willing and open for the purpose of knowing me and learning to love me for who I was, ethnically and culturally." She witnessed the way he was ready "to try something new, to move towards the unfamiliar, to approach me and the unknown with humility, tenderness, and bravery."[8]

Jun says that they laugh about how she's become more Asian over time. "The truth of it is that I've become more and more myself, and one of the most wonderful things about a good, safe marriage is the experience of being loved in the long, unglamorous, often painful, always awkward process of becoming whole."[9]

Even though she's married to someone white, she has felt safe enough and seen enough and free enough to step more fully into her Asian heritage. I feel similarly about my Black heritage. Experiencing the unconditional love of my husband has given me space and room to discover me. He doesn't criticize my whiteness but allows me to inhabit all that I am. I have friends like this, too, who are mature enough and wise enough and big enough to let me be me and enjoy what that looks like.

Your children need someone who will love them through the "often painful, always awkward process of becoming whole," and that includes racial and ethnic wholeness. If you are a person of faith, pray that your child will find someone who shares their faith. It's never too early to pray for your child's future spouse; I've been praying for my boys' future wives since they were born. Whether you're a person of faith or not, help your kids to understand the importance of being with someone who will seek to understand and love all of who they are, which includes their cultural heritage. The right person will not expect them to assimilate but will encourage them to step into every aspect of themselves.

QUESTIONS TO PONDER

1. Whom do you consider beautiful or handsome? Upon whom have your kids had crushes?

2. What diverse examples do your kids see of happy couples?

3. What kinds of conversations have you had with your teens and young adults about interracial dating?

4. If you are no longer married to your children's other parent, how can you try to make sure your kids don't associate dysfunction with that parent's color?

STEPS FOR APPLICATION

Toddlers and Preschoolers

—If you are a prayerful person, start praying for your children's future partners now! Pray that God will protect and watch over them and that your children will meet them in God's perfect timing. Also pray that they will love each other completely, including their racial and ethnic heritage, and that they will be a safe place for each other.

Elementary School

—Intentionally model mutual appreciation in your own marriage or relationships. Your kids will take mental notes on a subliminal level. Compliment your spouse in front of your kids and openly appreciate her culture.

Tweens and Teens

—Talk to your adolescents about the purpose of marriage and the blessing of being in a good marriage. Begin to teach them what they should look for in a boyfriend or girlfriend and ultimately in a spouse. If you made mistakes, share these with your kids, in age-appropriate ways. If you experienced a failed relationship or a failed marriage, tell them what you could have done differently. Did you fall for the good-looking one who had little character? If you are no longer married to your child's other parent, were cultural differences some of the reasons for the relationship's end? Make sure you don't pass racial prejudice on to your kids by suggesting that the problem with your former spouse was his color.

DATING, MARRIAGE, AND BEYOND   159

—Be honest about some of the challenges of interracial relationships but let your adolescents know that all marriages have challenges; their goal should be to find someone committed to them, which includes being committed to learn about all of each other.

—Teach your children discernment. Point it out when someone behaves selfishly, or foolishly, or callously. Show them what respect and responsibility and integrity look like. Their future spouse won't be perfect, but good character is the sine qua non. Without that, nothing else matters. A person's outside matters, but their inside—their heart—matters more. As God said to Samuel when looking for a king, "For God does not see as man sees, since man looks at the outward appearance, but the LORD looks at the heart" (1 Sam. 16:7b NASB). What are the traits that make a marriage a blessing or a curse? Jun writes, "True unity requires whole people, full of their colors—and hard, holy, humbling work."[10] Whoever your children marry, whatever their color, do your best to make sure they are up to this hard, holy, humbling work. That is the most important thing.

12

The Joy of Discovery

> I've been welcomed in both white and Black spaces since I was a little boy, but always understood that something about me made it such that I didn't fully belong in either. Race, obviously, was created as a social tool for power and oppression, and I don't quite fit neatly in any box. I feel no guilt about any of this. I didn't choose the conditions of my birth in 1979. I didn't choose to look the way I look. But it's all a part of me.
>
> —Activist Shaun King[1]

When I was a kid, I wished I were white. I'd drape a towel on my head and fling the corners behind my shoulders, pretending to be Cher. I loved my hair wet and dreaded when it dried and frizzed up again. I knew I couldn't identify as white; my brown skin would have made that ridiculous, but I didn't identify as Black either. Black, for the most part, felt foreign to me. When asked to check a box about race and ethnicity, I checked "Other" or simply left it blank. But no one wants to be an "Other" or a blank box forever.

And then one day I read in my Bible that I was planned and crafted deliberately. I also met beautiful Black women and began to enjoy Black friendships. I experienced within those friendships an acceptance, a generosity, an openness, and a warmth that lifted my soul. Those friends saw me and welcomed me in. I had grown up being very hard on myself, trying to fit in, trying to excel, and terrified by the prospect of failure. My Black friends kept telling me to just breathe.

I read African American authors and poets and heard in their words sounds I had never heard before. Their voices resonated deeply, and I felt as if I had discovered treasure, which had always been there, but just beyond my grasp. I became a Black woman, knowing that the world saw me that way, and I didn't mind that one bit.

But I went from being ashamed of my blackness to being ashamed of my whiteness. I didn't want to admit that I loved Chopin and Shakespeare. I was embarrassed by my poor attempts at Black vernacular, my stiff hips, and my ignorance of hip-hop. I went from wanting so badly to fit in with white folks to wanting so badly to fit in with Black folks. I lived in fear of being discovered, found out, that I was not truly Black. I had a serious case of imposter syndrome. The insecurity I carried from the unkindness of Black kids growing up put me on edge and made me want to closet the white in me.

Yet, it has been the steady drumbeat of acceptance from Black friends and from my husband that has enabled me to finally embrace being biracial; their love washed away the shame I bore from childhood. I'm sure there are Black people who still harbor a monolithic view of blackness, but my friends do not. I have a diverse community filled with mutual respect: friends who understand complexity, who know that few things are simply black or white.

I also had to acknowledge that the kind of trauma so many African Americans from my generation endured was largely foreign to me. I've been disrespected and called the N-word, but I was never herded into poor inner-city schools, nor did I grow up fearing police brutality. I went to the High School of Performing Arts (PA), made famous by the movie *Fame*, and then to an elite college, complete with a European study abroad. I have been spared much of the toxic racism that has wounded so many. I've also always had close white friends: men and women who were and are kind and generous and good. I don't carry the kind of deep hurt from white people that would make me wary or guarded around them, and that openness has granted me access into esteemed places. It took college and adulthood to find Black friends who didn't ostracize me for the privilege I have so clearly enjoyed and whose broad personal experiences themselves enabled them to make room for me.

Parents, when it's time to look at colleges or make post-high school plans, emphasize diversity when you counsel your children. Help them to see the importance of colleges or jobs that welcome and affirm BIPOC. Steer them away from homogenous environments, including colleges that lack diverse staff. The post-high school years are so formative and important to becoming grounded in an identity and worldview; try to make sure your kids have ample opportunity to meet a vast array of people.

Metabolizing how God saw me, finding acceptance by my peers, and forgiving my dad all worked together to help me to love myself. I also had to forgive my mom.

When children grow up witnessing an unhappy marriage, most blame one parent over the other. Few kids are sophisticated enough to know that fault often lies with both sides. They blame the obvious culprit and fail to realize things happen beneath the surface that make the other parent culpable too.

As I made Black friends, I wondered why my mom never made close Black friends. Her husband and children were the only people of color she knew on any kind of deep level. Why wasn't it obvious that we needed more people in our lives who looked like us? And why wasn't it obvious that we needed dolls that looked like us and books and magazines with illustrations of people who looked like us? When you marry a man, you marry his culture. Why did my mom seem so uninterested in learning about Black culture? She read all the time, but no books by Black authors. She had that initial conversation with the biracial man in the Black Elks Club, but there her inquiry seemed to end. It also seemed as if her anger over unmet expectations of my dad only added to his low self-esteem and only confirmed what his inner demons were shouting in his ear—that he was indeed not really a man.

However, over the years, I've learned to cut my mom some slack. I realized that in the sixties and seventies, there were few books and articles about interracial marriage, plus no internet and no affordable therapy. People didn't talk back in the day as they do now, but they held their cards more closely to their chests, suffering in silence, working, sleeping, surviving, and working some more.

Added to that, it was largely because of my mom that my childhood was rich in so many ways. Because of her frugality, she was able to provide countless piano lessons and better pianos. Her calculations made possible summer trips to the Canadian wilderness, a train trip to the Colorado Rockies, summer camp where I learned to swim and make a fire, and a Dartmouth education. Her ability to stretch a dollar meant Christmas presents under the tree and fancy holiday dinners. Moreover, she brought us to church, where I was introduced to the One who changed my life forever, and then she modeled spiritual disciplines like tithing, fasting, and daily Bible reading. Observing her ability to delay gratification helped me to delay gratification and practice the piano for thousands of hours over the course of my childhood and adolescent years. She brought me to PA for my audition and sat outside the room, praying for my success. She took my collect call from Dartmouth's Baker Library pay phone when I was weeping and terrified that I couldn't figure out a thesis for an English paper; she patiently listened as I described the book and then walked me through until I realized what I wanted to say. I can't imagine who I'd be without my mom.

As I have grown older, humbler, and more secure, I have been able to see and appreciate that there is a lot of my mother in me. I, too, am efficient, time conscious, and practical. Like my mom, I cook almost every night of the week. I'd rather walk than ride, and I always have a book on my nightstand. I hate being late, and I can be rigid, inflexible, and too intent on planning ahead. Jeans and black turtlenecks are the most I can muster for family photos, and I don't really enjoy shopping. I haven't spent hours at a beauty shop since my wedding day. That's my mom, through and through.

If I had daughters, I'm not sure that I would sit for hours braiding their hair either; hopefully we'd have the money to regularly take them to the beauty salon. Like my mom, I love being outside, and I expect my boys to go outside, on sunny and

THE JOY OF DISCOVERY

not-so-sunny days. Contrary to the beliefs of my old-school husband, I don't believe that being out in the rain or snow makes you sick. We live in the north, and if we went out only on nice days, we'd be inside most of the time—and that would be depressing.

I'm so proud of my mom's imprint on my life.

Thomas Lopez, who is white and Latino writes, "Forcing someone who is multiracial or multiethnic to choose only one race or ethnicity . . . when they identify with more than one, is an impossible choice. Imagine being in this position and asking yourself, which race is 'primary' in your life? It is like asking a child which of their parents they love more."[2]

I can't choose one anymore. I don't want to, and it's just not honest.

I also have a lot of my dad in me. I can converse with ease with almost anybody: rich, poor, Black, white, thick accent or not; it doesn't matter. I know a little about a lot of things and can keep up in most conversations. In the army choir, my dad sang with a rich, tenor voice. He owned the stage, and his presence filled a room. I, too, am at home on a stage. I can read people, drop one-liners, and find a rhythm without much effort. I used to love to play the piano, and now I love to speak and write. All are forms of communication, communicating a feeling, an idea, in a way that people will listen and understand. When I find my groove, I can stay there all day long. This natural ability to communicate comes from my dad.

I have been told that I have a great laugh, a disarming way, a warmth in my voice, an ease around people. Those are all from my father. I think food should be an opportunity for meaningful conversation. I like lingering over a meal, tossing around ideas, thinking out loud. All of that is classic Austin. I learned to spar from him, not with fists and gloves, but with words and ideas as we'd debate at the dinner table over politics and current affairs. (*Martin Luther King should have stuck with race; he had no business going after Vietnam. But Dad, that was such a terrible war! Yes, but it was Vietnam that got him shot.*) Those conversations sharpened my thinking, helping me to see issues from multiple sides. If I have any gravitas at all, it is from him.

Both parents taught me to be intellectually curious and intrigued by people, all people.

I don't know how many of these things are "white" or "Black." I don't know how many of them are cultural tendencies or personal tendencies. I just know that I inherited traits from both parents, and I'm grateful for that. I see value in all of it. If they both deposited tendencies and abilities in me, why shouldn't I identify with both of them? Why shouldn't I call myself biracial? Both parents were there when I was made; both parents made genetic contributions, some good and some bad. Both influenced me in tangible and intangible ways. Why would I want to deny either of them? They both made me. It has taken a long time for me to inhabit all of who I am, and it feels good to do that, at last.

Multiracial People Don't Want to Choose

I think the U.S. Census finally caught up to this reality in 2000 when it offered Mixed-race as a choice. An increasing number of biracial people resent being asked to choose one; we want to choose both because we are both. I know when I walk down the street, the world sees a Black woman, and I don't mind that at all. I am a Black woman who is also white.

For a long time, the one-drop rule prevented us from claiming both. Every form and every census funneled us into a box, whether we understood that box or not. Some wished to be as light as possible, rightly recognizing that often the lighter you are, the easier things will be. Others spurned any European part of their heritage, equating Europe with oppression and believing that acknowledging their white family would mean betraying their BIPOC family.

Both are bondage.

Kristina writes, "I just wish the world knew they don't get to tell multiracial people how we identify. Each of our own

THE JOY OF DISCOVERY 167

experiences is incredibly unique. . . . I absolutely would not change being mixed for the world."[3]

National Public Radio did a story about people who are Black and Mexican. As Mexican immigrants moved into Black neighborhoods in Los Angeles, the number of Mixed couples and Mixed offspring began to multiply. NPR spoke to Melissa, who looks completely Mexican but who feels just as Black as she does Mexican. She grew up eating grits and biscuits and hearing her dad talk about the civil rights movement. And she also ate carne asada and visited her mother's family in Nayarit, Mexico. She identifies as both, even though people who meet her assume she is completely Mexican.[4]

Some with whom NPR spoke have Black family members who have been assaulted by the police and Mexican family members who fear deportation. They're often asked to choose sides, but how can they? Both sides are in them, cojoined to create them.

When two cultures come together to form a child, one does not consume the other, making it null and void. Rather, the two come together to create something, someone entirely new. Parents, the child you created, no matter what she looks like, is the product of both of you. You were both there when your child was conceived. You contributed one set of chromosomes each. Even if your child looks more like dad or more like mom, it doesn't matter, and that may change over time anyway. When my husband was younger, he looked like his mom, but the older he gets, the more he looks like his dad. I'm sure most of us have witnessed similar phenomena. Eye colors can change, skin tones can change, hair texture can change. Basing ethnic identity on looks alone is simply too superficial.

Teach your children to be both, to love both, to inhabit both. The world will want them to choose one, but they don't have to choose one; they can choose both, or, if they are multiracial, they can choose *all*.

Remember, the motivation for racial categorization was oppression. God created the nations, and if your people hail from Africa, you will be dark, and if they hail from Europe, you will be light. It's fine to acknowledge that; it would be preposterous to pretend that this is not the case. But corrupt people grouped all light people on one side and called that side *white* and all dark people on the other and called that side *nonwhite* and then ascribed greater value to the white side. It took time for such a simple binary to fully form, but it did indeed form. At first, immigrants from southern and eastern European countries were not considered purely white and were therefore sometimes sent back. They were below northern Europeans but above everyone else. Some white folks even refused to take jobs traditionally held by Hungarians, preferring unemployment instead.

These "undesirable" immigrants soon realized that they had a choice: they could either assimilate into whiteness or be classified as people of color, and they knew which meant more privilege. One Serbian worker said during the era, "You soon know something about this country. . . . Negroes never get a fair chance." So they began to abuse Black people, and the more they did that, the whiter they became. They participated in restrictive covenants (the refusal to sell their homes to Black people) and in that way helped to make certain neighborhoods white only. By the 1950s, these immigrants were intermarrying, attending schools, and buying homes in places Black people never could.[5] They officially joined whiteness.

Black people can never join whiteness, and they shouldn't have to. This false binary is what we should disrupt and reject. Color is not random; it denotes ethnicity, and ethnicity is beautiful. Ascribing greater value to one color over another is random, and it is also wicked.

Your child has brown skin because part of his family descended from Africa, or the Taino, or Southeast Asia. And you should teach him about those lands, about the people from that side so that he steps into that brown skin with a smile on his face and a spring in his step. And his eyes are green, and his hair is straight because the other side of his family descended from Sweden. And you should teach him about that land and tell him those stories so that he can step into those European features with a smile on his face and a spring in his step, knowing that

THE JOY OF DISCOVERY

his European side is just as good as his non-European side, not worse and not better. The broader culture will try to convince him to abandon one, to be ashamed of one, to admit only one, and you have to teach him to joyfully step into both. It would be tragic if your child sees beauty and intelligence and innocence on one side and ugliness, ignorance, and criminality on the other. It's your job to make sure this doesn't happen.

If your daughter brings kimchi for lunch but can't speak Korean, the white kids may tease her about her food and the Koreans may tease her because she can't speak Korean. If your son likes soul food but can't hoop, he might experience racism from whites and rejection from Blacks. In other words, your kids may have a hard time fitting in somewhere.

Mariah Carey's 1997 song "Outside" talks about being biracial:

> Neither here nor there
>
> Always somewhat out of place everywhere
>
> Ambiguous
>
> . . . .
>
> And you'll always be
>
> Somewhere on the
>
> Outside.[6]

At some point, your children will likely feel as if they are on the outside. Our world loves to categorize, and your children defy categorization. Teach them to embrace the fact that they don't fit into a box and to relish in that. Their very presence disrupts the construct of race, and that is a beautiful thing.

Your children get to be leaders, to decide their identity, regardless of the perceptions of others. It takes courage to do this, because there are gatekeepers of every culture, and these gatekeepers try to decide who is Black enough or Hispanic enough or white enough or Asian enough to allow in. Yet Mixed people have to be both wise enough to know how they're perceived and confident enough to fling wide the doors and walk in, to bring *all* of who they are into a space, knowing they belong there. They should have the attitude, *this is part of my identity, whether you can see it in my skin (or language skills, or eye shape) or not.*

In an interview for my podcast *Let's Talk: Conversations on Race*, playwright Monique Franz talked about her biracial children's response to the police brutality of 2020. She said, "My kids were like marchin' around the house, just angry . . . enraged at the death of Floyd, going to every protest, organizing protests, carrying signs . . . and I was like, this is interesting! These kids are mad as hell! I was sensing this . . . biracial rage." Then Monique said that her son explained his feelings more deeply. He said that it really wasn't biracial rage, "It is the Black in me that is angry," he said. Monique added, "He just happens to have that biracial face so that some of his white friends will finally listen."[7]

That is so well said. It speaks to the powerful position of Mixed-race people. Like Esther, like Moses, like Daniel, and like Joseph of old, Mixed kids stand as a bridge between two (or more) cultures. A bridge can feel lonely unless they embrace that purpose and find friends who respect, love, and support them for who they are. Of course, that is not the only purpose of your kids; they have their own unique callings, gifts, and strengths to offer the world; they will be interested in and impassioned by different things. But if they truly step into *all* of their heritage, they will be open to all kinds of people and able to hear and understand and speak what others cannot. They'll know that white, Black, Asian, Hispanic people can all be kind and good because their mom, their dad, their grandparents are kind and good. They'll see cross-racial benevolence in more intimate ways than those who grow up in monoracial families, and God will use that to help bring healing and wholeness to this world.

In 2016, Ta-Nehisi Coates interviewed Barack Obama about his presidential run in 2008. Former President Obama admitted that he had doubts about winning, but then he added,

THE JOY OF DISCOVERY 171

What I never doubted was my ability to get white support. There is no doubt that as a mixed child, as a child of an African and a white woman, who was very close to white grandparents who came from Kansas, that the working assumption that white people would not treat me right, or give me an opportunity, or judge me on the basis of merit is less imbedded in my psyche than it is say with Michelle . . . I had as a child seen at least a small cross-section of white people but the people who were closest to me loved me more than anything and so even as an adult—you know if I walked into a room and it's a bunch of white farmers, trade unionists—I'm not walking in thinking, "Man I got to show them that I'm normal." I walk in there I think with a set of assumptions like "These folks look just like my grandparents." . . . And so maybe I'm disarming them by just assuming that we're OK.[8]

This is a beautiful illustration of the advantage your children have. Obama could bridge vastly different cultures because of his unique upbringing. Who will your children be able to disarm and relate to simply by being who they are?

Contrary to what Carey's song suggests, straddling two cultures, absorbing two cultures, doesn't have to be lonely. It can mean an incredibly rich, powerful life. Some will want your kids to place both feet firmly on one side; they will want to rewrite your children's narrative, but no matter. Your children, in partnership with their Creator, will write their own narratives, and those stories will surely be bestsellers.

QUESTIONS TO PONDER

1. Have your kids ever expressed feelings of being on the outside? What do they say?

2. How do your kids respond to racist incidents in the news? Do they identify with the victim?

3. How do your kids racially or ethnically identify? Do your kids understand why they look the way they do?

4. How can you help your kids fully identify with both sides of their heritage?

THE JOY OF DISCOVERY 173

STEPS FOR APPLICATION

Toddlers and Preschoolers

— Play a silly game with your little ones and ask them how they look like Mom and how they look like Dad. For example, do they have the same eye color as Dad or the same hair texture as Mom? Is their skin a combination of Mom's skin and Dad's skin? Teach them that this is fantastic! Mom *and* Dad made them, so they look like Mom and Dad, plus a little of Grandma and Grandad and lots of other people in their family. Help them to take pride in that.

Elementary School

— Help your kids to understand that they look the way they do because of gifts that both sides of their family gave them called *genes*. Read books about this to help them appreciate the wonder of it all. Here are some possibilities: *The One and Only Me*, by Arianna Killoran; *The Secret Code Inside of You: All about Our DNA*, by Rajani LaRocca; *God Made Me in His Image: Helping Children Appreciate Their Bodies*, by Justin S. Holcomb and Lindsey A. Holcomb; and *When God Made You*, by Matthew Paul Turner.

Tweens and Teens

— Celebrate your children's uniqueness and help them find friends who will celebrate it too. Talk to them about being a bridge. For example, if they are Black and Mexican, how can they help bridge those two cultures? Can they help their Black friends appreciate Mexican culture and disrupt any negative biases, and vice versa? Teach your kids about the incredible privilege of being a bridge builder and about the healing their very presence can bring.

Acknowledgments

Thank you to my beta readers; your thoughtful, wise insights were so helpful and appreciated.

Thank you to all who entrusted me with their stories; they added so much!

Thank you to my literary agent, Barb. Your suggestions, expertise, and encouragement were all welcome and vital to this project.

And last but not least, *thank you* to my editor at Westminster John Knox Press, Jessica. What a delight you are to work with! Thank you for believing in this project; your knowledge and recommendations made it so much better.

Appendix I
Discovering Your Cultural Values

Cultural values are passed on from one generation to another, sometimes intentionally and oftentimes subliminally. We acquire them through socialization; by growing up in a culture, we internalize the values of that culture. You and your spouse likely have different cultural values, and if one parent dominates the transmission of these values, your kids will grow up one-sided. For example, if your Mixed white and Chinese kids understand and appreciate only white American values, Chinese values will feel foreign and wrong, which means they will be less comfortable around Chinese people. That's unfortunate, because they are white *and* Chinese. For your kids to appreciate both sides of their heritage and feel comfortable with both kinds of people, they need to understand both sets of cultural values. They might not agree with everything on either side, but neither side should feel strange or inferior.

Here are six categories of cultural values for you and your partner to think about.[1] This list is by no means exhaustive, rather it is just meant to get the juices flowing. I bet some lightbulbs will go on, and you'll have plenty of aha moments as you learn more about each other. Once you've identified what you each value, decide together which values you want to pass on to your kids. It will likely be some combination of the two, which is wonderful! Your kids get to have the best of both.

1. Orientation to Time and Money

1. Are you future oriented or present and past oriented? Is it natural for you to save, invest, plan, and set

long-term goals, or do you tend to enjoy the moment, give time or money spontaneously, and set shorter term goals? For example, if you see something in the store you know your friend would love, how likely are you to buy it for them, even though it's an unplanned expense? Do you find it difficult to save money because you're often financially helping friends or family members? Do you naturally plan activities on vacations, or would you prefer waking up and taking each day as it comes?

2. How important is punctuality to you? If you are hosting a barbecue and you tell friends to come over around 5:00, are you expecting them to get there by 5:15, or is it OK if they arrive at 6:00—or later? Do you think it rude to arrive late to social gatherings?

3. Do you think you should have three to six months of expenses saved even if it means forgoing vacations, eating out, and buying new clothes until you've achieved that goal?

4. Are you naturally circumspect, or do you tend to let the chips fall where they may? For example, will you stay up late with friends, or will you think about how tired you'll be if you don't go to bed (and then go to bed)?

2. Being or Doing

1. Are you happy watching the world go by, listening to music, talking to people, or do those things feel unproductive? Does sitting still feel lazy to you?

2. How likely are you to stop and talk with a friend even if that throws off your schedule? How would you feel if a friend stopped by without warning?

DISCOVERING YOUR CULTURAL VALUES   179

3. Do you wake up with an agenda, even on weekends?

4. Do you feel unsettled if you don't have enough to do?

5. Do you mind if your kids stay in their pajamas all day during holidays or weekends?

6. Do you plan things for your kids to do during time off?

3. Individualism or Communalism

1. Does collaboration or working in a group come naturally for you, or do you prefer doing things solo?

2. Which is more important: individual rights or community? For example, do you think those without children should be exempt from paying school taxes?

3. Will you show up at a gathering out of obligation, even if you're tired, or will you decline, stay home, and watch TV? In other words, how often do you sacrifice your desires for the sake of other people?

4. Do you think about your family's reputation? Do you talk to your kids about your family's honor?

5. Do you pay your kids for doing chores, or do you expect them to do them for free?

6. Do you easily speak up if you feel as if you are being treated unfairly, even if the person is busy, or will you put up with the mistreatment because you don't want to bother them?

7. How involved are you in your children's decisions? For example, do you discuss what they wear, which electives they take, where they go to college, which major they choose, whom they marry?

8. Do you expect your kids to be independent by the time they're eighteen, other than, perhaps, paying for college? Do you expect them to call/text regularly, or is it OK if you don't hear from them for several weeks?

4. Expressive or Inexpressive

1. Do you highly value rationalism and try to communicate without showing emotion?

2. Are you uncomfortable around big emotions, like raised voices, loud crying, boisterous laughter?

3. Do you talk with your hands or keep your body still while you are talking?

4. Do you try to keep your voice even and soft, including when you're angry at your kids, or will you shout at them if you're angry? If you yell at them, do you feel guilty?

5. If a debate becomes heated, will you withdraw or keep going?

5. Authoritarian or Egalitarian

1. Do you often complain about how decisions are made?

2. Do you feel angry if you are not included in the decision-making process?

3. Do you feel disrespected if someone, including your kids, questions your decision?

4. Do you invite your kids to give their input into conversations or decisions?

DISCOVERING YOUR CULTURAL VALUES

5. Do you consider pushback disrespectful?

6. Are you formal with subordinates at work or friendly? Do you expect your kids to be formal with adults (using proper titles, such as Mr. or Mrs., etc.)?

7. How important to you is respect?

8. How democratic is your home?

9. Are your kids allowed to raise their voices in anger at you?

6. Certainty or Uncertainty

1. Are you comfortable trying new things and taking risks, not knowing how things will turn out?

2. Do you encourage your kids to take risks? For example, do you talk to them about taking a challenging elective at school even though they may fail, trying a harder ski slope, or biking down a steep hill?

3. Are you flexible and adaptable, or are you more rigid? How flexible are you with your kids? How thrown off are you when things don't go as planned?

4. Are you more likely to be prepared or to fly by the seat of your pants? Do you consider the latter disorganized or undisciplined?

Most of these values are problematic at either extreme, and one of the beautiful things about marriage is that often our partners come at life differently, which helps to bring balance and nuance to our lives. This is particularly true in interracial marriages.

Appendix II
Resources for You and Your Kids

Resources for You and Your Kids

American Desi, by Jyoti Rajan Gopal. New York: Little, Brown Books for Young Readers, 2022.

The Arabic Quilt: An Immigrant Story, by Aya Khalil. Thomaston, ME: Tilbury House, 2020.

Black, White, Just Right!, by Marguerite W. Davol. Atlanta: Albert Whitman & Co., 2019.

Blended, by Sharon M. Draper. New York: Atheneum/Caitlyn Dlouhy Books, 2020.

Eyes That Kiss at the Corners, by Joanna Ho. New York: Harper Collins, 2021.

For Beautiful Black Boys Who Believe in a Better World, by Michael W. Waters. Louisville, KY: Flyaway Books, 2020.

God Made Me in His Image: Helping Children Appreciate Their Bodies, by Justin S. Holcomb and Lindsey A. Holcomb. Greensboro, NC: New Growth Press, 2021.

Happy in Our Skin, by Fran Manushkin. Somerville, MA: Candlewick, 2018.

Honeysmoke: A Story of Finding Your Color, by Monique Fields. New York: MacMillan, 2019.

I Am Enough, by Grace Byers. New York: HarperCollins, 2018.

I Am Whole: A Multi-Racial Children's Book Celebrating Diversity, Language, Race and Culture, by Shola Oz. New York: Nielson, 2020.

I'm New Here, by Anne Sibley O'Brien. Watertown, MA: Charlesbridge Books, 2015.

Josey Johnson's Hair and the Holy Spirit, by Esau McCaulley. Westmont, IL: IVP Kids, 2022.

Mixed Me!, by Taye Diggs. New York: Square Fish, 2021.

More Than Peach, by Bellen Woodard. New York: Scholastic, 2022.

My Name Is Yoon, by Helen Recorvits. New York: Square Fish, 2014.

RESOURCES FOR YOU AND YOUR KIDS 183

No One Else like You, by Siske Goeminne. Louisville, KY: Flyaway
Books, 2017.
Other Words for Home, by Jasmine Warga. New York: Harper Collins,
2019.
Piecing Me Together, by Renée Watson. New York: Bloomsbury, 2017.
The Secret Code Inside of You: All about Our DNA, by Rajani LaRocca.
New York: Little Bee Books, 2021.
Unsettled, by Reem Faruqi. New York: Harper Collins, 2021.
We Are Not from Here, by Jenny Torres Sanchez. New York: Philomel
Books, 2020.
When God Made You, by Matthew Paul Turner. New York: Convergent
Books, 2017.
Where Are You From?, by Yamile Saied Méndez. New York: Harper
Collins, 2019.
Who I Am, by Susan Verde. I Am series. New York: Henry N. Abrams,
2023.
The World Needs Who You Were Made to Be, by Joanna Gaines. Nashville,
TN: Tommy Nelson, 2020.

Learning So That You Can Teach Your Kids

Articles

Sachi Feris, "One Hundred Race-Conscious Things You Can Say to
Your Child," *Raising Race-Conscious Children,* June 2, 2016.
Karen Tao, "10 Tips on Talking to Kids about Race and Racism," PBS
Teacher Lounge, June 8, 2020.

Books

Do Right by Me: Learning to Raise Black Children in White Spaces, by
Valerie I. Harrison and Kathryn Peach D'Angelo. Philadelphia:
Temple University Press, 2021.
How to Raise an Antiracist, by Ibram X. Kendi (London, England: One
World, 2022).
*Tell Me the Dream Again: Reflections on Family, Ethnicity, and the Sacred
Work of Belonging,* by Tasha Jun. Carol Stream, IL: Tyndale, 2023.
White Awake: An Honest Look at What It Means to Be White, by Daniel
Hill. Downers Grove, IL: InterVarsity Press, 2017.

White Lies: Nine Ways to Expose and Resist the Racial Systems That Divide Us, by Daniel Hill. Grand Rapids: Zondervan, 2020.

Why Are All the Black Kids Sitting Together in the Cafeteria? And Other Conversations about Race, by Beverly Tatum. New York: Basic Books, 2017.

Videos

"Children of Immigrants Share Their Experiences with Racism in Massachusetts," NBC News, November 13, 2023, https://www.youtube.com/watch?v=YMKsoYav_xg&t=2s.

1000% Me: Growing Up Mixed, directed by W. Kamau Bell, HBO Documentary Films in association with Get Lifted Film Co., 2023, https://www.hbo.com/movies/1000-me-growing-up-mixed.

"Racial Disparities in the Criminal Justice System," CBS 8 San Diego, February 17, 2021, https://www.youtube.com/watch?v=lxEoCQLhETg&t=34s.

"The Racist History behind the U.S. Racial Wealth Gap," Doha Debates, February 17, 2021, https://www.youtube.com/watch?v=aHkVvdPqvH4.

"Redlining and Racial Covenants: Jim Crow of the North," Twin Cities PBS, August 4, 2019, https://www.youtube.com/watch?v=ymOaiWla3DU&t=9s.

Notes

Chapter 1: What about the Children?

1. "Trevor Noah on Growing Up Mixed-Race in South Africa, 'A Product of My Parents' Crime,'" Howard Goldenthal, producer, *The Current*, CBC Radio, December 5, 2016, https://www.cbc.ca /radio/thecurrent/the-current-for-july-5-2017-1.4189847/encore -trevor-noah-on-growing-up-mixed-race-in-south-africa-a-product-of -my-parents-crime-1.4190666.

2. W. E. B Du Bois, *The Souls of Black Folk: Essays and Sketches* (New York: Blue Heron, 1953), reprinted with introduction by David Levering Lewis (Modern Library Edition, 2003), 5.

3. Tasha Jun, *Tell Me the Dream Again: Reflections on Family, Ethnicity, and the Sacred Work of Belonging* (Carol Stream, IL: Tyndale Momentum, 2023), 8.

4. Jun, xiv.

5. Vox First Person, "The Loneliness of Being Mixed Race in America," *Vox*, January 18, 2021, https://www.vox.com/first-person/21734156 /kamala-harris-mixed-race-biracial-multiracial.

6. Lisa Miller, "The Psychological Advantages of Strongly Identifying as Biracial," The Cut, *New York Magazine*, May 22, 2015, https://www.thecut .com/2015/05/psychological-advantages-biracial.html?fbclid=IwAR1YAvc _g0RTV96CFbD4hytlL9g0jHmzUwW438QdNbSLLb-GdFrRok9Rnno.

7. Miller, "The Psychological Advantages."

Chapter 2: Color Matters

1. Sam Briger, "Lenny Kravitz on Race, Being on the Road, and Ruff Ruff the Magic Dog," *Fresh Air*, NPR, October 6, 2020, https://wamu.org/story/20/10/06/lenny-kravitz-on-race-being-on-the -road-and-ruff-ruff-the-magic-dog/.

185

2. Tasha Jun, *Tell Me the Dream Again: Reflections on Family, Ethnicity, and the Sacred Work of Belonging* (Carol Stream, IL: Tyndale Momentum, 2023),133.

3. Jun, 121.

Chapter 3: Race, the One-Drop Rule, and Cultural Racism

1. Biracial in America Facebook Page, https://www.facebook.com /groups/429509987677248.

2. Jenée Desmond Harris, "The Myth of Race Debunked in Three Minutes," *Vox*, January 13, 2015, https://www.youtube.com /watch?v=VnfKgffCZ7U.

3. Ashley Montagu, *Man's Most Dangerous Myth: The Fallacy of Race*, 6th ed. (AltaMira Press, 1997), 58.

4. Montagu, 65.

5. Cotton Mather, "The Negro Christianized. An Essay to Excite and Assist That Good Work, the Instruction of Negro-Servants in Christianity, 1706," ed. Paul Royster (University of Nebraska–Lincoln, Electronic Texts in American Studies), 9.

6. Montagu, *Man's Most Dangerous Myth*, 73.

7. Erin Blakemore, "The Long History of Anti-Latino Discrimination in America," *History*, Sept. 27, 2017, updated Aug. 4, 2023, https://www.history.com/news/the-brutal-history-of-anti-latino -discrimination-in-america.

8. Department of State, Office of the Historian, "Founding of Liberia, 1847," https:// https://history.state.gov/milestones/1830-1860 /liberia.

9. Montagu, *Man's Most Dangerous Myth*, 72.

10. Steve Bradt, "One-Drop Rule Persists," *Harvard Gazette*, December 9, 2010, https://news.harvard.edu/gazette/story/2010/12/one-drop-rule -persists.

11. Beverly Tatum, *Why Are All the Black Kids Sitting Together in the Cafeteria? And Other Conversations about Race*, rev. ed. (New York: Basic Books, 2017), 303.

12. Tatum, 303.

13. Bradt, "One-Drop Rule."

14. Rob Picheta, "Meghan Reveals 'Concerns' within Royal Family about Her Baby's Skin Color," CNN, March 14, 2021, https://www .cnn.com/2021/03/08/uk/meghan-oprah-interview-racism-scli-gbr-intl /index.html.

NOTES

15. Blakemore, "The Long History."

16. Tatum, *Why Are All the Black Kids Sitting Together,* 86.

17. Elizabeth Sun, "The Dangerous Racialization of Crime in U.S. News Media," The Center for American Progress, CAP 20, August 29, 2018, https://www.americanprogress.org/article/dangerous-racialization-crime-u-s-news-media.

18. Doug Irving, "What Would It Take to Close America's Black-White Wealth Gap?" Rand Corp., May 9, 2023, https://www.rand.org/blog/rand-review/2023/05/what-would-it-take-to-close-americas-black-white-wealth-gap.html#:~:text=White%20Americans%20hold%20ten%20times,wealth%20inequality%20did%20not%20exist.

19. National Park Service, "Kenneth and Mamie Clark Doll," March 21, 2023, updated April 11, 2024, https://www.nps.gov/brvb/learn/historyculture/clarkdoll.htm.

20. Dixon Fuller, "Doll Test" YouTube, February 8, 2012, https://www.youtube.com/watch?v=tkpUyB2xgTM.

21. CNA Insider, "4- to 6-Year-Olds Review Dolls of Different Skin Colours," YouTube, March 30, 2022, https://www.youtube.com/watch?v=Q8_EqAWFs4k.

22. "How to Talk Honestly with Children about Racism," PBS Kids for Parents, June 9, 2020, https://www.pbs.org/parents/thrive/how-to-talk-honestly-with-children-about-racism.

Chapter 4: Colorism

1. Vox First Person, "The Loneliness of Being Mixed-Race in America," *Vox,* January 18, 2021, https://www.vox.com/first-person/21734156/kamala-harris-mixed-race-biracial-multiracial.

2. Ronald R. Sundstrom, "Kamala Harris, Multiracial Identity, and the Fantasy of a Post-Racial America," *Vox,* January 20, 2021, https://www.vox.com/first-person/22230854/kamala-harris-inauguration-mixed-race-biracial.

3. Victoria Vouloumanos, "Sixty-Two Mixed-Race Celebrities Who Have Actually Talked about Their Multiracial Identity," BuzzFeed, December 21, 2021, https://www.buzzfeed.com/victoriavouloumanos/olivia-rodrigo-naomi-osaka-who-are-mixed-race.

4. *1000% Me: Growing Up Mixed,* directed by W. Kamau Bell, HBO Documentary Films in association with Get Lifted Film Co., 2023.

NOTES

5. Luis Noe-Bustamante, Ana Gonzalez-Barrera, et al., "Majority of Latinos Say Skin Color Impacts Opportunity in America and Shapes Daily Life," Pew Research Center, November 4, 2021, https://www.pewresearch.org/hispanic/2021/11/04/majority-of-latinos-say-skin-color-impacts-opportunity-in-america-and-shapes-daily-life.

6. Jessica Wei Huang, "Colorism and Its Impact on Anti-Black Racism in Asia," *Medium*, August 23, 2020, https://huangjaz.medium.com/colorism-how-beauty-standards-are-strangled-by-western-ideals-ab8743cac8eb.

7. Rachel Hatzipanagos, "Latinos Have Many Skin Tones. Color ism Means They're Treated Differently," *Washington Post*, March 21, 2022, https://www.washingtonpost.com/nation/2022/03/31/latinos-have-many-skin-tones-colorism-means-theyre-treated-differently.

8. Noe-Bustamante, et al., "Skin Color Impacts Opportunity."

9. *Colin in Black & White*, created by Colin Kaepernick and Ava DuVernay, featuring Colin Kaepernick, Jaden Michael, Nick Offerman, Netflix series, October 21, 2021.

10. Buju Banton, "Love Me Browning," on *Mr. Mention*, May 6, 1992, Virgin Music Group.

11. "Colorism in Hollywood: Zendaya and Keke Palmer," *The Root*, July 26, 2022, https://www.theroot.com/keke-palmer-should-be-as-famous-as-zendaya-1849330451?utm_campaign=The%20Root&utm_content=1658857020&utm_medium=SocialMarketing&utm_source=facebook&fbclid=IwAR3xDXS31l899omg2hPFOnOU6pQMLxzpwJdg9RGTAWl6cV5pj1QD15mB0wQ.

Chapter 5: Cultural Shibboleths Matter

1. Kamala Harris, *The Truths We Hold: An American Journey* (repr., London: Penguin Publishing Group, 2020), 10.

2. Vox First Person, "The Loneliness of Being Mixed-Race in America," *Vox*, January 18, 2021, https://www.vox.com/first-person/21734156/kamala-harris-mixed-race-biracial-multiracial.

3. Michael Ahn Paarlberg, "Can Asians Save Classical Music?" Slate, February 2, 2012, https://slate.com/culture/2012/02/can-asians-save-classical-music.html#:~:text=%E2%80%9CMusic%20is%20a%20huge%20part,parents%20largely%20do%20not%20care.

4. Victoria Rodriguez, "In My Words: Navigating Feelings of Isolation as a Biracial Latina Who Doesn't Speak Spanish," opinion, *Daily Bruin*, March 2, 2021, https://dailybruin.com/2021/03/02/in-my

-words-navigating-feelings-of-isolation-as-a-biracial-latina-who-doesnt
-speak-spanish.

Chapter 6: You Can't Do It Alone!

1. John Donne, *Devotions upon Emergent Occasions: Together with Death's Duell* (1624), 31, triggs.djvu.org/djvu-editions.com/DONNE/DEVOTIONS/Download.pdf.

2. Stephanie Pappas and Callum McKelvie, "What Is Culture?" *Live Science*, October 17, 2022, https://www.livescience.com/21478-what-is-culture-definition-of-culture.html.

3. Rebecca Carroll, *Surviving the White Gaze: A Memoir* (New York: Simon & Schuster, 2021), 306.

4. Valerie I. Harrison and Kathryn Peach D'Angelo, *Do Right by Me: Learning to Raise Black Children in White Space*s (Philadelphia: Temple University Press, 2021), 50.

5. "Transracial Adoption: Statistics and Social Challenges," Online Degrees Blog, University of Nevada, Reno, https://onlinedegrees.unr.edu/blog/transracial-adoption-statistics.

Chapter 7: The Problem with Homogeneity

1. David Denicolo, "Meet Zoë Kravita: *Allure*'s June 2017 Cover Star," *Allure*, May 15, 2017, https://www.allure.com/story/zoe-kravitz-cover-story-june-2017.

2. Michelle Obama, *The Light We Carry: Overcoming in Uncertain Times* (New York: Crown, 2022), 103.

3. Obama, 96.

4. Tasha Jun, *Tell Me the Dream Again: Reflections on Family, Ethnicity, and the Sacred Work of Belonging* (Carol Stream, IL: Tyndale Momentum, 2023), 8.

5. Malcolm X, "Who Told You to Hate?" excerpt, Educational Video Group (Greenwood, IN: Educational Video Group, 1962), https://search.alexanderstreet.com/preview/work/bibliographic_entity%7Cvideo_work%7C2785586#:~:text=00%3A00%20Malcolm%20X%20Who,the%20shape%20of%20your%20lips%3F.

6. Allaya Cooks-Campbell, "What Is Code-Switching and How Does It Impact Teams?" *BetterUp* (blog), March 1, 2022, https://www.betterup.com/blog/code-switching.

NOTES

7. Taylyn Washington-Harmon, "What Is Code-Switching?" *Health*, updated January 4, 2024, https://www.health.com/mind-body/health -diversity-inclusion/code-switching.

8. Jun, *Tell Me the Dream*, 165.

Chapter 8: The Beauty of Diversity

1. Vox First Person, "The Loneliness of Being Mixed-Race in America," *Vox*, January 18, 2021, https://www.vox.com/first-person/21734156 /kamala-harris-mixed-race-biracial-multiracial.

2. Michelle Obama, *The Light We Carry: Overcoming in Uncertain Times* (New York: Crown, 2022), 137.

3. Chimamanda Ngozi Adichie, "The Danger of a Single Story," TED, October 7, 2009, https://www.youtube.com/watch?v=D9Ihs24 1zeg.

Chapter 9: Be Honest with Yourself

1. Vox First Person, "The Loneliness of Being Mixed Race in America," *Vox*, January 18, 2021, https://www.vox.com/first-person/21734156 /kamala-harris-mixed-race-biracial-multiracial.

2. Maya Angelou, Facebook post, January 11, 2013, https://www .facebook.com/MayaAngelou/posts/10151418853254796.

3. Ta-Nehisi Coates, *We Were Eight Years in Power: An American Tragedy* (New York: One World, 2017), 8.

4. Adrian Florido, "An Emerging Entry in America's Multiracial Vocabulary: 'Blaxican,'" *Code Switch,* National Public Radio, March 8, 2016, https://www.npr.org/sections/codeswitch/2016/03/08/467358961/an -emerging-entry-in-americas-multiracial-vocabulary-blaxican.

5. Phil Vischer and Lecrae, "Why Lecrae Is Still a Christian?" *Holy Post*, September 18, 2023, https://www.holypost.com/post/why-lecrae-is-still-a -christian-transcript.

Chapter 10: Be Honest with Your Kids

1. Karen Valby, "The Realities of Raising a Kid of a Different Race," *Time*, n.d., https://time.com/the-realities-of-raising-a-kid-of-a-different-race.

2. Shane Wiegand, "History of Segregation and Racist Policy in Greater Rochester," n.d., ca. 2010, 19, https://landmarksociety.org/wp-content /uploads/2019/05/ShaneWiegand_Redlining-Segregation_web.pdf.

NOTES

3. Heidi Shin, "I'm Helping My Korean-American Daughter Embrace Her Identity to Counter Racism," *New York Times*, March 19, 2021, https://www.nytimes.com/2021/03/19/well/family/Talking-to-children -anti-Asian-bias.html.

4. Manuel Bojorquez, "That's When I Expected to Be Shot," *CBS News*, August 25, 2014, https://www.cbsnews.com/news/alex-landau-after -denver-police-beating-thats-when-i-expected-to-be-shot.

5. Shin, "Helping My Korean-American Daughter."

6. Valerie I. Harrison and Kathryn Peach D'Angelo, *Do Right by Me: Learning to Raise Black Children in White Spaces* (Philadelphia: Temple University Press, 2021), 112.

7. *Cleveland Clinic,* December 5, 2021, https://my.clevelandclinic .org/health/articles/22192-puberty.

8. Bill Chappell, "After Police Killing of Unarmed Man, Tulsa Chief Promises to 'Achieve Justice,'" *The Two-Way*, National Public Radio, September 20, 2016, https://www.npr.org/sections/thetwo-way/2016/09 /20/494697359/after-police-killing-of-unarmed-man-tulsa-chief-promises -to-achieve-justice.

9. Samaria Rice, "Tamir Rice Safety Handbook," *ACLU*, November 2019, https://www.acluohio.org/sites/default/files/ACLUofOhio_Tamir RiceSafetyHandbook_2019-11.pdf.

10. Claude M. Steele, *Whistling Vivaldi: How Stereotypes Affect Us and What We Can Do* (New York: W. W. Norton, 2010), 7.

11. Russell Contreras, "Rate of Latinos Killed by Police Skyrockets," *Axios*, May 30, 2023, https://www.axios.com/2023/05/30/police-brutality -latino-george-floyd.

Chapter 11: Dating, Marriage, and Beyond

1. Ronald R. Sundstrom, "Kamala Harris, Multiracial Identity, and the Fantasy of a Post-Racial America," *Vox*, January 20, 2021, https://www .vox.com/first-person/22230854/kamala-harris-inauguration-mixed-race -biracial.

2. Katharine Chan, "Let's End the 'Undesirable Asian Male' Stereo type," *Very Well Mind*, May 23, 2022, https://www.verywellmind.com /let-s-end-the-undesirable-asian-male-stereotype-5271703.

3. Chan, "Let's End the 'Undesirable.'"

4. Nhari Djan, "The Woes of Being a Black Girl in an Online Dating World," *Popsugar*, May 4, 2020, https://www.popsugar.com/love/what -its-like-to-be-a-black-woman-on-dating-apps-47327074.

192 NOTES

5. Djan, "The Woes."

6. Ravi Mangla, "The Race Dynamics of Online Dating: Why Are Asian Men Less 'Eligible'? *Pacific Standard*, October 22, 2015, https://psmag.com /social-justice/why-are-asian-men-less-eligible-on-tinder.

7. Meghan Markle, "Meghan Markle & Mariah Discuss Their Biracial Identities," *Archetypes* (podcast), August 30, 2022, https://www.youtube .com/watch?v=9--5-EfzjzU.

8. Tasha Jun, *Tell Me the Dream Again: Reflections on Family, Ethnicity, and the Sacred Work of Belonging* (Carol Stream, IL: Tyndale Momentum, 2023), 59–60.

9. Jun, 60.

10. Jun, 25.

Chapter 12: The Joy of Discovery

1. Shaun King, Facebook post, May 23, 2021, https://www.facebook .com/photo.php?fbid=330148801807700&set=p.330148801807700&type =3&ref=embed_post.

2. Thomas Lopez, "I Am Latino, I Am Also White: Why a Latino of Mixed Ancestry Struggles Each Time He Fills Out a Form," *LAist*, December 4, 2020, https://laist.com/news/race-in-la-latino-white-multi racial-multiethnic-mixed-ancestry-thomas-lopez-masc.

3. Vox First Person, "The Loneliness of Being Mixed Race in America," *Vox*, January 18, 2021, https://www.vox.com/first-person/21734156/kamala -harris-mixed-race-biracial-multiracial.

4. Adrian Florido, "An Emerging Entry in America's Multiracial Vocabulary: 'Blaxican,'" *Code Switch*, National Public Radio, March 8, 2016, https://www.npr.org/sections/codeswitch/2016/03/08/467358961 /an-emerging-entry-in-americas-multiracial-vocabulary-blaxican.

5. Brando Simeo Starkey, "White Immigrants Weren't Always Considered White—and Acceptable," *Andscape*, February 10, 2017, https://andscape.com /features/white-immigrants-werent-always-considered-white-and-acceptable.

6. Mariah Carey, "Outside," track 12 on the album *Butterfly*, Columbia Records: September 10, 1997.

7. Nicole Doyley and Monique Franz, "Interracial Marriage and Biracial Rage," *Let's Talk: Conversations on Race* (podcast), May 11, 2023, https://www.youtube.com/watch?v=vUQ-5ORJHLA.

8. Ta-Nehisi Coates and Barack Obama, "The Making of a Black President," *The Atlantic,* December 14, 2016, https://www.youtube.com /watch?v=SosrjYPr8ss.

Appendix I: Discovering Your Cultural Values

1. Adapted from "Cultural Values," CareQualityCommission, May 12, 2022, https://www.cqc.org.uk/guidance-providers/adult-social-care/cultural-values.

www.ingramcontent.com/pod-product-compliance
Lightning Source LLC
Chambersburg PA
CBHW050101190125
20506CB00031B/341